José Mauricio de Carvalho

Living the meaning

José Mauricio de Carvalho

Living the meaning

Freedom, belief and hope

ScienciaScripts

Imprint

Cover image: www.ingimage.com

This book is a translation from the original published under ISBN 978-3-330-76226-8.

Publisher:
Sciencia Scripts
is a trademark of
Dodo Books Indian Ocean Ltd. and OmniScriptum S.R.L publishing group

120 High Road, East Finchley, London, N2 9ED, United Kingdom
Str. Armeneasca 28/1, office 1, Chisinau MD-2012, Republic of Moldova, Europe
Printed at: see last page
ISBN: 978-620-8-08510-0

Summary

Preface

With this short book of reflections, Jose Mauricio de Carvalho adds another work to his vast output as a philosopher concerned with our reality, both locally and globally. His aim is to address the way in which we build meaning into our lives and thus gain the ability to live more authentically. He does this by discussing the various situations and themes that pervade our existence in this world, such as immersion in time, relationships with others, family life, coping with social change, faith, the problem of God, work, freedom and dignity. Despite the complexity of the issues dealt with, the language is accessible and clear, making it easy for the reader, who does not need to have a philosophical background to follow the arguments. Among the discussions presented, we highlight the one on the construction of meaning in life (Chapter 5), where we believe the reader will feel more challenged to rethink their own existence based on the questions posed by Jose Mauricio. The questions of faith and God should also provoke those readers less inclined to religiosity. In discussing the problems, Jose Mauricio mentions the names of the authors who have inspired his reflections, such as Jaspers, Ortega, Julian Marias, Heidegger and Viktor Frankl, encouraging the reader to look to them for further elements to enrich their future reflections on the burning issues dealt with here. At the end, Jose Mauricio states that there is still a lot to say about these issues, thus recognizing our incompleteness as human beings. But he also establishes two certainties: that our future is unpredictable and that, in the face of the great changes we have experienced, human beings still have the task of finding a reason to live. It is up to the reader to immerse themselves in reading this book in order to understand and experience the philosophical and existential challenges it presents.

Paulo Margutti

FAJE

Introduction

Considering what life is seems inevitable. It is what we are in our relationship with the world. It may be more or less intense, more or less meditated upon, more or less loved, but it is our very existence. We live in what we do, especially in our choices. Not everyone gives their choices the attention they deserve, but they are what weave our existence. And why not? Because of the natural difficulties of life, the tribulations that overtake us, the pain that penetrates us, the rush of our days, the illusions of a happiness that is offered as a purchase or sale, the great haste that is far from being the urgency of living. And then there's the lack of self-knowledge and the lack of concern for the meaning we want to give to the adventure we are.

In order to deal with the problems of survival and well-being that we strive for, man has created science and technology, and they have become indispensable and very demanding to learn. That's why it's a task that almost everyone undertakes from an early age. Learning a science or a technique is the main challenge of our time. Parents teach us from an early age that being a good professional is a prerequisite for success. And they are right both to say that science is fundamental and to worry about their children becoming professionals. This is often compounded by a concern for physical and psychological health, and there are language classes, gymnastics, swimming and fitness classes alongside regular schooling. The best parents still devote themselves to loving conversations with their children. Many do this successfully, but this is the grandparents' task par excellence. The latter touch on the issues discussed below, but we don't know how successfully or intensely. The point is that, in our time, finding meaning in life seems difficult.

Science is not all we do, there are other things we need such as art, religion and philosophical meditation. But modern science has gained more visibility because its success is enormous in controlling nature and it is very pleasing to be in control of the world. In short, what do we do when we create all these cultural manifestations and experience so many loves and lives?

The essentials for living come from living. Some things we learn by looking and talking, others we learn from ourselves. With our mistakes and successes. In order to understand life as a fabric that we make every moment, it is essential to learn how to go into the future. And this creation is also an art, or a distinct form of art for which science, religion, philosophy and the cultivation of beauty are of great help. But this magnificent art of living is an opening to the future. An opening that means leaving behind something that may have been magnificent, but that hasn't exhausted our purpose of loving, of exploring the possibilities of living, of fulfilling every hope of experiencing something good, not necessarily pleasurable. This force that moves us forward, guided by an internal compass, is what we understand to be meaning. Meaning is what moves us and will move us well if we are attentive to this intimate compass. This is what the Spanish philosopher Jose Ortega y Gasset masterfully called intimate fidelity. By dedicating our lives to doing things, we'll have a life that's more like our own if we do it with respect for the direction that our inner compass points to.

Looking forward is what stabilizes our journey. It resembles the experience of the cyclist who only remains balanced while pedaling and moving forward. The cyclist can stop and/or go backwards, but not with the same speed, intensity and impetus as when launching towards the finish line.

What we are going to deal with in this little book is meaning, that something that drives us forward, something that makes living worthwhile. It is meaning that nourishes hope for the future of man, of the personal man and of humanity. We understand that the construction of this personal meaning is part of the process of creating humanity, which only takes place in the small existences that give rise to it.

And in filling in the meaning we come across situations and issues that populate existence, and we'll talk about them in the chapters of this book.

1 Living in time

There are many ways of describing life. We can start with this one: living is fulfilling a journey through time. Not a ready-made script, a story already written, like the character in a soap opera. A journey with human characteristics, of course, not in the same way that a sheep, a bee or a tree live. If we say that human life is not like that of other beings, it's because there is something different about moving through time. When you go to school, to work, to meet your friends, or even when you go on holiday, existence is made up of choices and activities. Man does not stand still, his existence is dynamic and this movement is a construction of meaning, as we will see below, an experience of freedom.

Movement in existence also has a different characteristic from freedom or the construction of meaning when we look at it as the result of biological and material processes. Our existence has a material aspect and this reality has its own dynamics of aging, a process that biological science is uncovering in greater depth every day, starting with the genes that formed us. We are, however, more than a body, we have life, a psychic soul and a thinking spirit. We also have a personal history that we live in the greater time of a culture.

We live as a whole; our body, psychic and spiritual consciousness change over the years. We are these transformations, what we become. It is a process that involves these strata of existence, but it seems that the process that affects the body can more properly be called ageing. In other words, psychological and spiritual consciousness also change over time, but we can't say exactly that they age. Aging is a more appropriate category to describe the wear and tear of the body. Our body is the basis of psychological and logical experiences, it supports our presence in the world, it situates us in time and space. It also presents us to others. It is the transformations that affect the body over the course of a lifetime that are more akin to ageing. The problem is that the wear and tear on the body affects the other layers of our existence. In some way, physical wear and tear compromises psychic and logical functions, but psychological and spiritual objects don't age. Living, from this biological perspective, is aging, although living is also about other things, as we'll see in later chapters.

As we live in a body, we age. There is another important characteristic of the category of aging. Aging applies to changes in matter, but better refers to the transformation of living beings. We can talk about old rocks, old landforms, old stars, but this is a derivation. Aging refers to matter, but its most precise use is to characterize a living being.

Treating life as a process means that in order to understand a person, we need to know their history. It also means that we don't die at any given moment, that death is not an episode contrary to life, but that we are constantly changing and dying. Death is part of the process of becoming. So is growing old. Dying, when it doesn't happen to young people too soon, comes with the decline of strength and health, a kind of arrival point. It is the moment when dreams come to an end, when projects are interrupted, when hopes and achievements come to an end. However, death is not always predictable and this gives life a dramatic character. Things don't always turn out the way you expect them to; many things happen to us in life.

We've come to another way of describing life. Living is what we do in the time of our lives. And what we do when we are forced to choose. Ortega y Gasset said something important about the meaning of this doing in *Ensimismamiento y alteration* (1994): "Man's destiny is therefore primarily action. We do not live in order to think, but on the contrary, we think in order to continue living" (p. 304).

Our freedom is limited, our ability to choose is between the alternatives we are given. Our choices are never absolute. Some complain about this, but choosing between possibilities is the way to live human freedom. And there is a great risk in this: we can lose our humanity. Ortega said something like this: "Man is never really man, but to be man means precisely to be on the verge of not being man" (id., p. 305).

Considering the choice in the circumstance, life takes the direction of those choices made. They shape the existential fabric of which we are made. We are not made of choices that have not been made and paths that have not been traveled. What could have been is not our past. The time we have lived makes us unique, even though we have so much in common with other people. And the longer we live and the more aware we are of our choices and the existential path we are following, the more we perceive ourselves as unique. Thus, every man who dies is a world that is gone, a world that is lost, a wealth that cannot be recovered. When each man dies, he takes with him a world of experiences and lessons learned. And if life is the result of what we do, of the choices we make over time, lived existence is an art. In this art there are involuntary marks, life is also made up of what happens to us.

In this journey through time, what is most truly part of me are the things done, the loves lived, the dreams realized, the paths built, the work left behind in what has been externalized. A little of who we are remains in what we do. And what we leave behind is what enables future generations to move forward. The new generations receive things from the previous ones. That's what isn't lost, but it's not much. What we are in our entirety is lost.

At no other time in history has mankind lived the average lifespan that we are reaching at the beginning of the third millennium. This means that, as humanity, we have more time to carry out the work of meaning that is living our existential singularity. It's hard to say how much longer this process can be extended, but the lengthening of our days on this earth has changed many things in recent years. A longer existence forces us to consider more seriously the essential changes we have undergone. Our formation process is lengthening and so is what we can accomplish.

The aging process we talked about at the beginning is this journey through life. Someone may go through several fundamental changes. Each person's journey is unique. It seems that at least two major changes mark life in our time: at the end of adolescence, the first lines of our own existential territory are established. This is when everyone begins to understand that there are things that are important and others that are not so important. Before, we already knew that some things we liked, but this knowledge was intuitive. We just liked or disliked what was happening. Adolescence is different: we identify with certain things. They speak of us and not to us. A dancer's dance, for example, can tell me something, not just because my friends say it's interesting, my parents say it's delicate, my teachers say it's art. Dance can mark my existence, I begin to identify with what appears there, I am a bit of that or not, regardless of whether I have taken dance steps. I begin to realize that my life is mine because I appreciate things or not. This is also how I dress, how I see myself. I no longer do it for others, but for myself.

The dawn of adulthood is the initial moment of our singular affirmation. We already have an identity. We are more rational or emotional, more logical or intuitive, more or less affective. We know that this is who we are, or at least we have an inkling of it. Choices, what has happened to us and what we have inherited have made us this way, they have tied our existence together. This is the moment when we make significant choices about our profession, love and friends. It's the time when we make important decisions that we hope will last a lifetime, but which we find difficult to carry through when we have another big moment of change. There is no exact date for the second big change, it could be at forty for some, fifty or even sixty. It's the lengthening of life that allows us to lengthen this second time of change.

This second great moment of transformation establishes a review, not just any review we do every day, but a really deep, intense, transformative review. Now it's no longer a question of asserting oneself singularly in front of parents and friends, but in front of oneself, the young person we were and are no longer. It's time to take stock and confront ourselves. At this point, many things that seemed important at the beginning of adulthood no longer are, and many things that seemed irrelevant become indispensable. The love of youth, true, sincere, warm, may not withstand these changes, the profession chosen with the help of the best psychopedagogue may no longer satisfy. This is the time when successful professionals leave everything to set up an inn in the mountains or a bar on the beach. Many beliefs change with the passage of time or with things that happen to us. If some choices survive such changes, it's because what came from the past has also changed, the profession has brought other compensations, the love of youth has reinvented itself. Note that this is not about staying with your partner out of laziness, convenience or convention. A new encounter is being established. It seems that it's just not possible to go through life without encountering these challenges. Some dare to face them, others are unable to do so.

And in order for existence not to be a fabric of many patches and seams that have little to do with the rest of the cloth, each choice needs to be made responsibly, i.e. considering the whole. However, it seems inevitable, at least for most men, that some breaks will be made. And we need to learn to deal with these ruptures, to live them without guilt, to reduce the negative effects of our choices and to move forward responsibly. Taking care of ourselves and the people around us.

We can go through important changes in life, essential discoveries. Realizing that we are limited and finite, wanting to do something that we don't think we can, but that we would like to, are all part of this learning process. These powerful experiences become part of our lives and stay with us, gaining a relevance we never imagined they would have. There are many important occasions that change our existential trajectory, but none of them have the dimension of the two indicated above. On these two occasions we gain a new profile, it's not something that has changed in us, it's us who have changed.

As life gets longer, we need to be more careful with our choices. We will have a longer time to make them. Choices are tied together in a kind of vital fabric and we often find ourselves tied in the middle of life to commitments from our youth that we can't carry forward. This discovery can mean a hard time of crisis, a time to change or die.

In this period of radical change that takes place from the middle to the end of life, depending on the necessary breaks, it seems that we will no longer be able to live or will have no way of moving forward. We often plunge into death, not necessarily physical death, but the existential death of a job that no longer enchants, of a relationship that no longer seduces, of routine and boring occupations that no longer give meaning to our days. Only intimate fidelity, the trust in life itself that springs from who knows where, suggests that it is possible to continue living on new horizons. We discover that life has not yet come to an end, there is more to do if we don't get stuck in our past, if we get rid of the existential traps that have been created and bind us. At this point, we discover that we haven't achieved everything yet, that we still have a way to go before the body collapses, that we need to do more to complete our existence. If you go through this process of renewal well, the increase in life expectancy and the opportunities that have arisen are a new chance to live. It will be time to redo some things.

This extension of life does not diminish the anguish of death. The awareness of death always accompanies us and the fear of what we don't know is inevitable, as well as the suffering, pain and limitations that usually precede it. These limitations become more visible with the increase in the number of elderly people in society. The presence of so many older people highlights the limits of our lives.

The extension of life has presented this generation with the challenge of extending productive time, working more before retirement and doing other things after retirement. This is inevitable because with the increase in life expectancy and the number of old people, nations consume a growing part of their income to pay for pensions.

Contemporary societies are faced with the challenge of living with a growing number of elderly people who are limited in their ability to work, move around and take part in society. At the same time, the reduction in the birth rate is reducing the number of young people available to work for these social groups. This is a reality that we will have to live with in the coming years. This is a phenomenon that is spreading among the world's major nations, the lengthening of life spans and the reduction in the birth rate. It has changed the profile of the social pyramid in many parts of the world.

The need to work a little longer before retiring is not a bad thing. Many people retire and continue to work. Being active is a good way to renew challenges and improve income. However, at some point you have to stop if you don't die first. Imagining a life that extends into very old age working and being fully active is an illusion. The notion of eternal work is one of the painful myths of our time, an unnecessary burden to carry. As we get older, we find it difficult to maintain productive activity. Worse still is the inification of ageing that has become popular in recent years. Today we hear about the wonders of living in the third age, known as the best age.

Every age has its charms and challenges, but mystifying old age is not a good way to live with it. Neither is false acceptance, manifested in expressions that a person looks very well and young, a good strategy. Mystification is a disaster because it treats existence as what it is not. We need to know that our existence ends, it is marked by finitude. There comes a time when you can no longer have a child, there comes a time when you can no longer see without glasses, there come days when you can no longer work efficiently. There is a time to live each stage.

The consequence of the myth and mystification, fed by economists and governments, is to extend retirement requirements in a world where people are expected not to stop working. Despite the myth of eternal work, man will stop, he hasn't changed biologically from what he is. And while medicine has managed to increase people's average lifespan, the real limits are no different from those of the last few generations. Many of our grandparents lived into their 80s, 90s and even beyond. Finding out what to do in the final years of existence is a unique experience, it depends on many factors, but it will be good if we can continue to create and make choices that artfully finish the fabric of existence.

The average life expectancy is a statistic that applies to the men of an era. It doesn't guarantee a long life for all of us, least of all for me, it just raises the expectation of a longer life for more people. They will have a few more days to complete their art. And this expectation of living a few more days shows the possibility of doing something different: of creating more technology or science, of living art or religion, philosophy or literature in a different way, but above all of improving relationships in the various dimensions of love.

Life takes on the dimension of eternity if the meaning constructed in our daily work contributes to human culture and remains for future generations. If what we live and leave behind makes us present to future generations. This is the way to remain, in the music we composed, in the poem written and recited in the future, in the books written, in a technique developed, in short, in everything we manage to leave as an objectification of what we were. However, what we leave behind doesn't change the fact that the concrete existent is permanently undergoing a process of wear and tear and will come to an end as a subjective reality.

2 Discovering the other

We learn to deal with the world through our experiences of it. The way the world appears to me is the way it really seems to be, but we're never sure that it really is. We believe it to be so, or rather, modern Westerners that we are, we have learned to treat it that way. The world seems to be something to me and I try to confirm these impressions by exchanging information with other consciousnesses that represent it. Through the exercise of communication, we end up convinced that our way of understanding the world represents it well and that it is well as we experience it. It's a belief that helps us to live. This belief is not just that of an individual, but of a society. This way of thinking is a construction that we have learned from the generations that came before us.

Historians of Western thought have found the roots of the formation of subjective consciousness at the end of the Renaissance. The French philosopher Rene Descartes was the one who managed to express that what the man of his time saw, everything he felt, everything he heard and what reached the subject was not simply exteriority, as had been thought until then. In fact, many generations, from ancient times until the 17th century, imagined that this was the case. It seemed to them that things existed outside of us and somehow came into us. Descartes showed that it was impossible to be certain if we remained in such an understanding. The process might not end well and the world might not show itself properly. So Descartes made personal consciousness the locus of our certainty. Whereas ancient man was outward-looking, Descartes treats pure intimacy as the space of certainty. I think, and in the depths of myself, I discover myself as a being in the world. And as a being in the world, I can relate to things and to other consciousnesses. I think, therefore I exist. The discovery of subjectivity, presented in the fourth part of the *Discourse on Method*, appeared to Descartes:

> so solid and so exact that not even the most extravagant suppositions of the skeptics could shake it. And so believing, (he said) I concluded that I should have no scruples about accepting it as the first principle of the philosophy I was seeking" (DESCARTES, 1978, p. 66/67).

This extraordinary discovery by the French thinker changed the way we think. However, this marvelous discovery of Descartes, this turning point in the understanding of reality, which cannot be disregarded once it has been discovered, ended up leading to exaggerations. The body itself was no longer something that could be thought of as other, what we know of it is an idea, a representation of what it really is. Knowing how consciousness forms its understanding of itself and of things and how it deals with the world has occupied generations of men since the beginning of modern times. And through the process of exaggerating what delights because it shows us what is wonderful, life itself and everything that surrounds it, consciousness has been reduced to thought. Descartes doesn't understand that the world can enrich consciousness; on the contrary, it becomes isolated. And the result of isolation and loneliness is an awareness of singularity that is, of being one and different from everything else. But subjective consciousness in this way is a solitary seat.

If this Cartesian discovery has bequeathed us great things, if we have learned that our knowledge of the world refers to our own way of knowing it and dealing with it, if the experience of ontological solitude somehow still seems valid, modern man has learned that he cannot reduce the world to the contents of consciousness. And this process and the accounts it contains have many implications and chapters. I don't need to describe it in detail. It's enough to note that, in any case, this great self that grew so much until it became Absolute, in the formula given to it by the German philosopher Georg Hegel, had to be reduced to its true size by the philosophers who followed him.

We are a singular world, we experience our surroundings and place them at the edge of our consciousness. We open ourselves up to our surroundings and discover that what exists does not fit into our thoughts. However, that which is beyond subjective consciousness is never fully revealed within it, because it has aspects that go beyond it, even though they appear within it. The material stratum that makes up this world is something impenetrable and, since it is impossible to know it intimately, we have developed science, which has established various methods of studying and describing it. We then learned to quantify and represent what is impenetrable to us.

We are learning to live with it, the world seems like something to us and we only understand it that way, but it has aspects that are not limited to what appears to our consciousness, that is, it has something that goes beyond what we experience.

And among the many things that go beyond what we perceive, beyond what we imagine, is the other. This other is more than we are capable of thinking, it never fits in with what we expect. However, this other subject is not an absolute stranger in the same way that matter is in its most intimate composition. Matter escapes our grasp, although we can have a representation of it and describe it through the laws of science. Physics gives us such a representation.

This other person who isn't me, but who has something in common with me, can teach me many things just because they share impressions and knowledge with me. It's another person who is different from me, but with whom I can exchange impressions.

We are born into a family, we belong to a national society, in other words, we are born into relationships. Right from childhood, many of us experience the unpleasant tightness in our cheeks, especially when they are red and round. People love round cheeks and squeezing them is like saying: welcome to the group. And so we enter society, the cheek squeeze is a modern form of social initiation, although not an exclusive one. It's the other who emerges in front of me to squeeze my cheek as a sign that he recognizes us. We are welcome. It's the other who also gives gifts, who smiles, who strokes, who rejoices in our childish antics.

As we grow up, relationships take on new meaning. Others are no longer just a source of satisfaction or dissatisfaction, classified according to whether they relieve our needs, distract us or annoy us. Others have names, are located in space, establish relationships of trust and teach us how to deal with our surroundings. We learn to name things, we learn to think with the group, we learn to use the group's linguistic references to describe what is happening to us and around us.

Discovering the other is fundamental to our relationship with the world. We discover that the other doesn't always meet our expectations, doesn't always do what we expect and often does what we don't want. The other is freedom and action, it is different from things that work regularly. If we turn on a computer, it offers the programs we have installed, the clocks mark the hours according to their mechanism, the lamp turns on when we press the switch and the filter purifies the water. If these things don't work as expected, it's because their mechanism has become corrupted. However, the other is not like that, it can do something different from our expectations without being corrupted. How difficult it is to deal with what we are in the other, how difficult it is to learn that others also have a unique script of existence. We have learned to call this freedom, an experience we have also lived.

And so, when we distance ourselves from the symbiotic relationship with our parents and acquire autonomy, we discover that this other person doesn't hinder our existence with his freedom; on the contrary, he helps me to get to know myself. He teaches me patience, asks me to overcome my egoism and allows me to build my uniqueness in these relationships. This is a huge challenge in our time, because somehow modern subjectivity has come to be experienced as absolute individuality. Individuality distanced from others, individualism shaped by solitude. And it is in this way of living in a society where technology acts as a barrier to closeness that individuality becomes loneliness. These are aspects of the human contradiction: communication technology, which has expanded contacts around the world and accelerated global exchanges, also works to keep real people apart.

This is the challenge of our century: to rebuild intimacy. Not the closeness of banal conversation or superficial relationships that hide what we truly are, but the encounter capable of bringing love and friendship to life in the encounter. The encounter in depth, in the hope of a good expectation, because when we are able to experience the other as other, we discover what we are, we realize our uniqueness, we go through our interior, but we don't dive into isolation.

This other who appears to me is gendered, he is male and female. I'm only referring to the way he feels and presents himself so as not to get into the unnecessary polemic of homosexuality, which means nothing in an in-depth encounter. And although men and women have social roles that have been defined in the development of societies, they have shaped unique behaviors that seem natural to them. Such is the feminine whim in the ornamentation of the body and the home, the dedication of women to their children, or the masculine effort in the development of technology and control of the world. Just as we avoid the polemic of genres, we want to avoid the relationship between the sexes as subordinate or exploitative. In fact, throughout history, human relations have often been guided by the exploitation of slavery or female subordinacy. However, what we hope to highlight in the encounter with this other is the wonderful experience of love. This is one of the most important dimensions of the relationship, the discovery of the other as an object of love.

With the beloved comes a community of affections, desires, projects and shared dreams; with him or her, life gains flavor and joy. And from the joy of love between man and woman, children are born. In recent years, this central nucleus of social love has been changing its profile, but it doesn't matter what transformations the family goes through. It can have fewer children, the partners can worry about personal and professional development, they can bring children from other relationships or adopt them. If they live in a community of love, the loved one will offer the most important experiences of tolerance, dedication and surrender. And in discovering the children that arise from conjugal love, we have very enriching experiences, because these others are not an extension of us, nor of our projects, but they are still part of us, even though they are different from us.

Children teach us better than other people that human relationships are not completely alien, although they are not limited to what we think or want them to be. Love for our children is a good example of the love we can develop for other people. Jesus said that even those who do evil can give good things to their children. And so it is, with children it is possible to have a good experience of love.

Family relationships bring the presence of this other into my world. If their desires conflict with mine, it is this other who most profoundly changes my existence and the course of my instincts. He is not only the member of my family, he forms a tangible community of destiny with me. What happens to him affects me, his pain also bothers me. He builds pages of the future when together we choose the future of our group. He allows me to live the experience of transcendence, which is only possible beyond me because we share a common humanity.

And among the others in the world, you can discover an extraordinary Other. Not everyone does, but a huge number of people identify him. As a society, we have learned to call him God (however we understand him) because he is not like the men and women we know. However, the biblical experience that has formed our cultural tradition and our reason shows that we only come to this great Other through the men and women we meet face to face. Perhaps God is, like matter, truly Other, because our similarities are insignificant given his transcendence, but if we work under the inspiration of the belief revealed in the Bible, then we have something of this God deep within us. He is not a complete stranger.

Human relationships have many dimensions - legal, political and sporting are just a few examples. However, it is the experience of love that gives personal relationships their densest and most meaningful reality. Because love breaks with the rules that are written and agreed to make life easier, love revolutionizes relationships just as it revolutionizes the rules. That's why Jesus of Nazareth was rejected in his society because his love for others didn't fit into the existing rules. Love brings the possibility of renewing rules and concepts, but this is very difficult to experience.

3 Family life

There are many forms of relationship in society, as we mentioned in the previous section. And of all the close relationships, those of love are the most significant. They include friends, close people, professions and even national groups. In a broad sense, we can speak of a love for humanity, but the most visible expression of human love is that which is experienced between people who love each other and, by extension, in the family nuclei that they form.

And family love is an important part of human relationships. Much of who a person becomes is due to what they learn in the family, and many of their most significant experiences are lived in the family. The family is an important social organization.

Family organization has changed throughout history, but we are living in a time of profound transformation of the family institution. Everything is fast. Different generations living together in our time experience these changes differently. It's clear that older people living today will find it more difficult to understand the changes than young people. That said, exceptions will always exist to confirm the rule. How difficult it is for so many people to understand the movements that are taking place in families and to discover new forms of love in the process. It will be even more difficult to do so while remaining within the framework of the traditional family, the model established by husband, wife, children and close relatives. However, the family relationship as an expression of love is not limited to the patterns of other times, it is renewed with creativity and freedom, without ceasing to be present in more conventional forms.

And we start with what is difficult in the changes of our time. Love relationships are not limited to set patterns and old models. Love can spring up in many ways. It asks us to overcome selfishness, to be able to go beyond ourselves and give ourselves in ways we don't even know how. There are many people who entered into relationships with little conscious love in their youth in order to please parents, friends or relatives, or even people who, as their lives changed, discovered new dimensions of love, redefined intimate demands and ended old relationships.

We might ask: doesn't love have the dimension of eternity? Don't people who love each other feel that this love lasts for eternity? It seems that way. In an autobiographical text, Karl Jaspers wrote something like this about the love he experienced with Gertrud Mayer:

> From the time he was a student, she surrounded him with boundless love, not consenting to insincerity, firm in her demands. As if they had found each other in this world from an unimaginable other, as if they remembered each other without knowing it, they lived, with infinite gratitude, the daily reality of their lives, throughout the unstable years, for more than half a century (CARVALHO, 2006, p. 254).

It seems that it is a love like this that Jesus said would last forever (Mt 19:9). Such a love is what God created from the beginning of creation. However, this love with a sense of eternity is far from being limited to formal commitments, to unions made to meet family demands, to nuptial agreements made out of fear or insecurity, to relationships that mean little or nothing to the couple. In these cases, there seems to be no love with a sense of eternity.

Some of this confusion about permanence has its origins in ancient Greece. There, the notion of definitive love was mixed with the idealization and separation between the material world and that of eternal and perfect ideas. The experience of eternal love that we are describing does not even have the sense of eternity described in the Greek tradition. Placing the life lived under an ideal means disregarding reality, what one feels and what the other is has no reality, the relationship is expressed in an archetype of perfection that does not translate the reality felt and lived. In Plato's ideal of perfection, things on earth should conform to the model of what is beyond experience. Idealization doesn't always translate the experience of surrender and going out of oneself, the experience of dedication and surrender that makes the common humanity grow in the two who love each other. And such unities are not what God envisioned, they have no dimension of eternity.

And the Greek influence, its incorporation into Christian thought, led to a lack of concern for the body. Today, we are witnessing a reverse movement that is being reborn with all due exaggeration. The body cannot be neglected or put aside, but neither does it exhaust man's reality. Love can only be experienced in the various strata of human life, a life that needs to be taken as a unity in the materiality of the body, in the vital processes that take place in it, in the affections experienced and in thoughts.

It seems that overcoming idealization is gaining momentum in recent generations, and idealization in personal relationships really needs to be overcome. The problem is not to make the rules simpler for separations, the problem is to realize when marriages are fulfilling the love they should be fulfilling. Christianity, contaminated by Platonism, has lost what is essential and followed the path of pain. And often, in the name of a wonderful principle of love, we try to force relationships that don't really exist. How can you keep people together who don't love each other, who don't want to remain a couple? Is that God's will? Is this God's plan for the man he created? Or is God's will for people to be fulfilled in marriage, to discover the meaning of love that opens up in its fullness in living together.

Changes in the way we live and the secularization of society have opened up space for separations. The number of new unions has increased, leading Western society to finally admit divorce, or at least to deal with it better and accept new family relationships. The new era contains opportunities, but it is no guarantee that we are heading in the right direction. Marriages that are not well grounded in love have failed in the past and will fail in the future. What is not structured on love cannot be forever. Starting with sexual activity, which today is not always experienced in the sphere of marriage. This circumstance has at least served to avoid using marriage as a way of legitimizing sexual relationships. That was done in other times. Sexuality should be good in marriage, but you don't get married to legitimize sexual relationships. Condoms and contraceptives have brought greater freedom in sexual relationships, and couples are freed from unwanted pregnancies and sexually transmitted diseases. In this new reality, couples can build experiences of intimacy that are good for them.

Sexual intercourse is not just for reproduction, as Christian leaders of the past thought. They did this by assuming Aristotelian positions. In doing so, they lost the dimension of man's unity and reduced sexuality to its most visible function: reproduction. However, sex is more, it is an experience of surrender and acceptance. It allows people to feel welcomed by others, to express their affection and to experience care. All this is important for a happy life. There are those who are happy in celibacy, but in relationships of love, sexual life is an important reality not only for reproduction, but for what it represents in personal development.

Sexual life today is part of a historical era that treats sexuality as broader than the sexual act. Desires have to do with the historical organization of society. We don't have sex like we used to; what we do depends on the historical experience of our group. Sex needs, among other things, to be consensual, to be experienced as freedom, to be an expression of affection, to be a moment of welcome. It doesn't make sense to have sex like the cavemen, it doesn't make sense to drag your desired woman around by her hair like in the movies from the caveman days. Sexual life is part of man's historical reality and cultural development.

Before dealing with the significance of love as a structuring factor in family relationships, let's explain a little more about the changes taking place in family organization. As far as family movements are concerned, there have been many changes in recent decades: birth control has reduced the number of children, women leaving the labor market has forced changes in domestic activities, knowledge of the psychology of children and old age has increased the demands of caring for children and the elderly, and new forms of authority have been established between parents and children. The book *Etica* describes these and other changes that the family has undergone:

> The family, for example, has changed a lot, the moments spent around the table, the weekend get-togethers have been substantially reduced, fathers and even mothers are trying to reconcile family life with professional achievement, women are preoccupied with physical beauty and men are trying to earn more money to meet new consumer demands. All of this brings changes that we need to understand and evaluate. There are consequences we don't want, such as the absence of parents for long periods of time and the lack of affection in families, as well as indebtedness to maintain growing consumption. Immature children prolong their stay in the parental home until very late ages compared to when the previous generations began their independent lives. If you look at women's competition with younger women, you can see the desperate and unfortunate attempt to look younger than they are. Of course, there are also exaggerations in the behavior of old fifty-somethings who look like irresponsible teenagers competing with their grandchildren on dating sites, although this phenomenon seems less important socially than women's preoccupation with appearance. More visible is the exaggeration of the fifty-year-olds, regulars at beauty clinics, plastic surgeries and gyms, the Botox generation, competing with daughters and granddaughters with their legs and bellies showing. All this points to a world of horizontal family relationships, with reduced authority, where parents want to be like their children and not the other way around (CARVALHO, 2010, p. 167/168).

And in the changes that families are going through, today's men and women are concerned with individuality, and this concern has repercussions on the family nucleus. Greater attention to singularity has repercussions on women's greater independence and the growing concern with the professional training of both sexes. The result is a reduction in the amount of time family members spend together.

This is the reality of families today, so little can be said about where family organization will go in the future, how homosexual relationships will be consolidated, for example, and what space they will have in society. What will happen to future generations if they don't incorporate values, respect norms and authorities? We're not sure in what terms this respect will take place? We are in the midst of change, and what seems fundamental is that organizations depend on the way in which everyone assumes their lives and makes choices. Relationships will not be eternal because they have to be or should be, they will have the dimension of eternity if they lead people to a full life, if they help people to mature and feel happy together. They will only succeed if they allow people to experience love. There's no certainty that the new times will lead to this, but that doesn't mean it can't.

Love is opening up and discovering the other. Another person who never shows themselves completely, but who enchants with every new face they show. This other is someone with whom you have important experiences, a companion in life, in projects, dreams and achievements. Love lived in this way resembles the experience of prayer. Prayer also opens us up to the Other, and prayer also changes our personal lives. It is in the space of freedom and otherness that love grows and fosters personal growth.

There is nothing idealized about the relationship described in this way. It can, but it doesn't have to be eternal, it doesn't have to be definitive because love is ideally definitive. Quite the opposite, it won't be permanent because it represents perfect love, it will be permanent if it is born of love and it won't be if it isn't born. It won't be permanent if love has no sense of the future, if it doesn't experience the joy of the future to come.

Love lived in the future dimension is a source of personal renewal. Those who live it find new reasons to do things, enrich their personal world and broaden their concern for others (or others when it includes children, friends and relatives). Love is based on the hope of improving one's life, of overcoming personal limits through forgiveness and being forgiven, overcoming the circumstances that diminish each individual or couple. And this relationship of love is consolidated in the truth, the truth of each person and the truth of the relationship. Love does not flourish in lies, simulations or concealment. Somehow the hidden is revealed, it shows itself in a slip of the tongue, in an exchanged word, in an unwanted glance. It's in the gospel that nothing remains hidden, which has been confirmed by psychology. You can't pretend all the time.

There is no love in possession. Aristotle treated women as possessions of their husbands. Many times in history, women have been regarded in this way. It doesn't matter if it's a man or a woman, if the other person is a possession, they are an extension of the owner and not someone you love. Love liberates, it does not enslave, in slavery and dependence there is no love.

A family can stay together without love, but it will lose the main thing. The routine may work, the children may go to school, the parents may work, the food may arrive on the table, the clothes may be in the cupboards, but there will be no space for intimate growth and affection. Without them, people don't feel supported in their limitations, they don't overcome them, they don't grow, they don't rejoice.

True love is something that man should not and cannot separate, it is not common and will not be easily found in every family formed yesterday or today. This love is uncommon, but it is what counts, it is what matters, it is what makes human life good. Love that does not lead to personal development is not love.

Let's free ourselves from bureaucratic relationships, from meaningless sex, from routines that are not open to transcendence, from a future without hope, from life without love. It is in love that we have the best chance of happiness; it is in the relationships of true love that we can experience eternity and transcendence.

4 A changing society

Family life is not what it used to be. We talked about this in the previous section. The patriarchal family of a hundred years ago has been radically transformed. It has changed because science has advanced, society has changed and problems have become different. Women started working outside the home, the pill and other condoms made it possible to plan pregnancies, men and women became more concerned about their own individuality. None of these changes are good or bad; they express a different time. However, what we do with them can be one or the other. If individuality, for example, means getting to know ourselves in order to know what is good for us, to discover what we can do with less effort, to understand what makes us happy, it's good, but if individuality means becoming selfish, incapable of understanding others, incapable of forgiving, incapable of living together, then it's bad. And human coexistence is not easy. No one is perfect, even the people we love the most have limitations. Among other things, we have to consider that everyone's difficulties and virtues end up being affected by the way in which social relations take place, by the way in which society is organized.

We saw in the previous chapter that there is no way to keep social institutions immune to social change, nor is it desirable to do so because new challenges require new responses. On the other hand, it is unreasonable to idealize the past because nothing human is perfect. Things can get better, although there is no guarantee that they will. Huge families, economic difficulties, authoritarian fathers and the submission of women were all problems in patriarchal families. There was a lot to change, but there was also more time together, more affection, a greater presence of the mother and more sharing. There was a huge sense of belonging and families didn't dissolve easily. The new families are challenged to respond to the new times, but to maintain the love, welcome and human respect that generally existed in the old families. Putting these values back into the new ways of living as a family is a challenge for today's generation. It is necessary to seek the implications of personal uniqueness and professional fulfillment that are challenges of our time, but to preserve the hours of conviviality, being around the table, eating the baked cake together. Living these values in relationships that are less violent but no less respectful, relationships where parents don't shy away from giving guidance and children feel the strength and affection of this guidance. Encourage relationships where parents are role models for their children and don't want to be like them. The issue here is not dignity, which equals all men regardless of age, but experience and responsibility, because fathers will always be fathers. They have more life, more experience and the mission to feed, guide, educate and protect their children. They need to find new ways of educating so that their children want to be like them.

Families don't organize and change outside of society. They are born and change in the social space. That's why much of what families are, how they organize themselves and how they deal with their problems depends on what's going on in society. Those of you who were born in the middle of the last century, like me, lived in a world divided between capitalists and socialists and in a country run by an authoritarian government. In those days it was easier to know what was right and what was wrong, even if the choices were not preceded by sufficient critical analysis. The communists and anarchists were wrong. Western liberal society was right. We had to be home by ten o'clock, and our parents didn't go to bed until we'd returned from the movies or meeting friends. Apart from a few nonconformists, no one complained. And because of the lack of criticism, it wasn't difficult to change positions quickly. Many people who supported the government of the '64 revolution changed their minds over time. For the supporters of socialism, capitalism was the source of all evil and for the defenders of the free market, socialists were the cause of all the evil in the world. The world had a right side and a wrong side. And among Brazilians, capitalism seemed right, but it was never assumed to be good. Those who defended the authoritarian government said that every protest or demand was unpatriotic anarchy and every action in support of the government was correct. Over time, Brazilian society changed and two decades after the revolution began, what seemed good was no longer, simple as that.

There was no deep debate about why something was or wasn't the way it was, but over time, and in the superficiality of a society without debate, democracy began to seem like the solution to all ills. The exiles returned and tried to find a place in that society. Many of them became political leaders, others leaders of social movements.

We moved to a time of fluctuating truths like the movement of a seesaw, sometimes something was true, sometimes the opposite. There was no possible dialogue, we still didn't deepen the political debate. At least in our country. Even so, things changed, authoritarianism brought difficulties when it came to solving problems. On the world stage, the dispute between communists and capitalists ended as no one had imagined. We knew for sure that the world was heading for a terrible war, there was the fear of the atomic bomb and what it would cause. This was a universal fear and not just ours. Karl Jaspers, one of Germany's most respected voices, even said at one point in his book *The Atomic Bomb and the Future of Man* that (1958, p. 12): "it was possible to bring about the total destruction of life on earth by the very action of man." That was the feeling.

The desire for universal peace grew. The hippies proclaimed peace and love. Despite the recognized human instinct for destruction, man began to desire it:

> the structuring of the environmental world, the obtaining of the means necessary for present and future life, the achievement of a full life through peaceful competition, the vision of beauty and meditation on truth, should no longer be replaced by the tiring and ruinous activity that stems from the destructive impulse directed against the fullness of life (JASPERS, 1958, p. 33).

There was a certainty that Soviet totalitarianism would only be destroyed from the outside, since a totalitarian system could not be fought from within, but despite this belief, the Soviet Union disintegrated internally like a sand castle, impoverished by an inefficient economic system and a corrupt and oppressive political elite. In short, the socialism of human justifications and beautiful ideals was a corrupt government and an inefficient economy.

Against this backdrop, philosophers began to say, get busy renewing the future, don't despise reason and have the courage to do what it takes to change the world. And Jaspers said what this courage was (1958, p. 47): "to always do what is possible, both in knowing and in not knowing the course of things, and not to abandon hope while living."

However, the fear of complete annihilation has taken us from the hope and rationality intended by Jaspers to a different and equally dark side. Fear has made us desperately anxious, immediate and hedonistic. We begin to occupy ourselves especially with the present and with what gives pleasure. Immediate pleasure only takes us over completely when we lose the dimension of happiness, and I think that's what we've lost at the turn of the millennium. We are no longer sure that we can be as happy as we would like to be. And in these days of transition, we have experienced a sense of crisis, of change, of transformation. And we have seen the emergence of another mass man, more consumerist, more hedonistic, more immediate than Ortega y Gasset's mass man, but with those characteristics that he identified still intact: satisfied landlord, spoiled child and ignorant expert.

What is certain is that the world is different today than it was fifty years ago. A lot has come from there, but there is no longer a visibly evil side, there is no longer a right or wrong form of government. Ideologies are on the wane. Everyone wants good results, but few get them. There's a globalized world and democratic governments almost everywhere, a single world, but it's become difficult to see what's right and what's not, it's not easy to distinguish in this society at the beginning of the millennium which goals to strive for. It's not easy to understand the logic of the urban violence that dominates our cities and many cities around the world, the strength of the drug trade in some regions of the States accuses the governments of poor countries. It has also become difficult to understand today's wars: what does the Islamic State want with the barbaric killings and terror it imposes? What to do with the mass migration of those fleeing the war in Syria, Africans arriving in droves on the Italian Peninsula or Latin Americans wanting to go to the United States? Even Brazil has become a target for Haitian and African migration. Where there is peace and a little development, it has become a place of search for desperate people with nothing. There is not so much fear of the big bomb, but small conflicts are spreading all over the world, multiplying violence, terror and barbarism.

It has become difficult to correct bad behavior or an antisocial act, considering that a slap from a parent, regardless of the intensity or circumstance, can be criminalized. Virginity, so highly valued until recently, has become trivial and worthless. The world of families has become complicated not only because of what they have to face, but also because of the profound changes in the environment in which they live and where they feel no sense of security, a world where jobs are not guaranteed, peace is always under threat, urban violence surrounds every door and terrorism is a constant threat.

The world has become a village. What happens in one corner is watched in real time in every corner. The effects of what happens in one place soon reach everyone, or almost everyone. All these changes have not come about because world trade has intensified, but it is advancing. Trade has been increasing ever since the discovery of America and the great voyages to the Orient.

There is enrichment, but not necessarily social and human progress. Wealth is not distributed. Human growth and development, when it occurs, is not progressive. It is not today as it was not yesterday, but there was a time when we believed it would be. There are peaceful periods in history and troubled ones. There are times when trade intensifies and governments are strengthened, and there are periods when the movement is reversed.

Brazil has been part of this global market since sugarcane was planted to produce and export sugar, a process that was accelerated when the Minas Gerais mines started producing tens of kilos of fine gold, much of which was taken to Europe to finance palaces and public investments. Let's not think that the essential thing is to condemn the collection of taxes by central governments - some people did that in the past. Attributing Latin America's backwardness to the plundering of European metropolises was the prevailing discourse in the so-called third world. This discourse has gone out of fashion. They were partly right, but they didn't consider the enormous local progress brought about by the auriferous exploitation that created a marvelous complex of roads and towns. All of this today is not an economic alternative for many communities because we Latin Americans have never been able to preserve our historic cities as we should, to recover and rebuild them when necessary and to organize a flow of tourism capable of sustaining investments. It's a pity, because tourism is growing all over the world, especially in Europe, where entire cities are being rebuilt and historic sites are being renovated with great ease, without the bizarre debates that our preservationist authorities are having. We don't even realize that architectural styles are dated creations, but aesthetic achievements are timeless or that human works are all destined for destruction if they are not redone and/or well preserved. It's even worse when we don't understand that a people's history is the root of its cultural identity and that a people's identity is also found in its monuments.

In the last century, the world market has changed with the revolution in communications and the intensification of trade. Families have been lost in the cultural standardization spread by the media, the universalization of shoes, clothes, musical tastes, dances and the world of work. It seems strange that young people all over the world are queuing up to attend the same musical events. Companies now have the whole planet as their consumption horizon and produce the same type of product for this global audience. Families and their members need to move around in this new social space and each person is challenged to find the necessary elements for their choices.

In the third chapter of *The World-Culture,* entitled *The World as Image and Communication,* Lipovetsky and Serroy deal with the reception of this globalized trade. They note the preference for global products. They say (2011, p. 113) "It is in this context that we are witnessing the advent of a transnational consumer who wants the same brands everywhere and behaves according to the same standards". They observe a certain standardization in the way of life in the world's major cities, which are coming closer together (id., p. 116): "in a kind of globalized homogenization of products, consumers and culture." The reception of this standardization is not without resistance from local references who try to preserve their own style, as is the case with typical dishes or the national currency, but it is a movement of adaptation to change. All over the world, local designers are metamorphosing (id., p. 117): "traditional dress codes into a modern style and contribute to the advent of a global fashion based on the rehabilitation of roots, of ethnic identities." The authors say that the process of globalization of spending is not limited to offering standardized products such as Coca Cola, but promotes an increasingly diversified offer, bringing trends and products from one corner of the world to the big chains. They clarify (id., p. 119): "Zara, say the authors, renews its models every two weeks, producing around 12,000 *designs* every year." The expansion of supply accelerates the differentiation of individuals who seek a very particular profile within societies. There is a particular reception of world habits where particular aspects dialog with those of world culture, one feeding the other. And, also against the backdrop of disorientation, hedonism and loss of ethical references, we see the emergence of movements and reactions that reactivate core and traditional cultural values. At this point, the authors recognize in Western values the elements that can serve as a reference for contemporary man. They state (id., p. 135): "the sense of moral indignation has by no means been eradicated, our societies reaffirm a stable core of shared values: human rights, honesty, respect for children, rejection of violence and cruelty."

If the process of globalization of the economy has gained momentum since the end of the Second World War and communications have turned the world into a kind of village where everyone speaks to each other, we have also mentioned movements to defend local culture. They have been affected by trade, the communications revolution and the popularization of the internet. It seems difficult for many people to realize that the world still has real borders, even though electronic media and commerce seem to be unaware of them. However, despite what Lipovetsky and Serroy mention, in the face of the Syrian refugees marching desperately towards Europe, national borders are visible in ever larger fences and increasingly hostile receptions. The same can be said of the way Latin Americans are received in the United States. In a world with a globalized economy and global products, borders still resist and national societies perceive themselves as culturally distinct. These groups find themselves challenged to forge links and establish new bases for old concepts of belonging. The differences between groups remain, but economic integration is promoting changes in local cultures.

At the end of the book, Lipovetsky and Serroy mention the attempt to organize a more humanized world order. To this end, they mention the recovery of values such as discipline and merit in schools, combining aspects of the current teaching model with elements of the old pedagogical system seems to be a good way forward in the authors' assessment. Another aspect they highlight in building this civilization is the construction of (id., p. 161): "a general culture, transforming what is no more than a disorganized heap of information into a body of knowledge and shared values." In addition to these initiatives, universities need to be reinvigorated in what is most significant for the formation of critical consciousness, giving it back (id., p. 165): "its first and irreplaceable mission: to form man." It also seems important to them to review the cultural policy that spends huge sums of money on the state to cater for a small elite. They also consider it necessary to recognize ecological values and struggles against minorities.

Although it can be said that the core values of the West - the human person, freedom, the rule of law and democracy - remain firm, a world civilization does not seem to be taking hold. Or rather, there are so many differences between the richest and the poorest, between Western countries and Islamic societies, that it is difficult to speak of a common civilization. The borders of national states resist and the gap between rich and poor widens. What happens is that communication networks reduce the ideological control of poor societies. This is because people contact each other directly without the mediation of powerful groups and official government positions. The internet has made it possible for people from different countries to contact each other directly and say what they think.

Global economic exchanges have led to the emergence of economic blocs which, despite their differences, are reshaping relations between states. Thus, we see countries that were rivals until recently (Germany and France) now defending common interests and other nations that were once close (European countries and former colonies) moving apart.

So we're in a moment of transition where the big corporations have their own interests, which don't always coincide with their states of origin. However, they still maintain their headquarters in their countries of origin and take the bulk of their profits there. On the other hand, faced with the growth of international trade and the intensification of world trade, national governments strive to preserve local markets and take protective measures to defend them. The less strong these national governments are, the more they fail in these attempts. Furthermore, the market and trade do not reduce social inequalities within countries any more than between them. Those who are well prepared for the new era undeniably benefit from the new developments, but those who fail to follow the logic of this process remain outside it and further away from the economic and technological vanguard. In poorer countries like Brazil, rich, industrialized areas like Sao Paulo benefit more from world trade than the interior of the country and the northeast, for example. It is a time of transition in which the face of the new world is showing, but the old one is not over yet. However, the world that is emerging is not going in the direction pointed out by Lipovetsky and Serroy.

It is in this world that families move, and it is there that each person will build the meaning of their life. It is in the space of families and society that people are formed and live. That's where they make their choices and give direction to their lives.

5 Weaving meaning into life

One of life's most important lessons is that it only seems interesting when we live for something worthwhile. We call that something meaning. To live is to build meaning. It doesn't seem possible to have a good life without giving it meaning, i.e. living in the day-to-day routine of what to eat, what to wear and where to sleep. It's not that there aren't people who simply work and live for small diversions and passing pleasures. However, life doesn't look good stuck in the past and the present. It should also be borne in mind that, in days like ours, routine work, which is less and less creative, but no less absorbing and tiring, doesn't seduce anyone.

On this point, some existentialists are right. Living according to a vital project, seeking something and having faith in the future modified according to aspirations and vocations, is not a secondary aspiration, something we may or may not cultivate. To live according to a project is to look to the future as an overcoming of what binds us to the past. If there is pain that prevents us from loving, if there are fears that make it difficult to try, if there are limits that close the doors to happiness, it is necessary to change this present. Not to live this possibility is to despise our freedom. A present without a future is nothing more than the reflection of a limiting past, but our existence contemplates the possibility of being different from what we were. This being different in hope and effort is the meaning, the other name of freedom.

The construction of meaning requires awareness of what we are. It's not possible to know what to do without knowing ourselves well, lost in routine and trivia, without thinking about ourselves and what we'd like to do. Not that we can do without work and routines, these things are important for the comfort and well-being of society. The problem is that this is not enough for a good life.

The task of self-knowledge requires daily moments of meditation. Once it becomes a habit, this reflection points the way forward. It is important and shows how some things seem good, others not so good. It also helps with self-knowledge for professional counselors. Psychologists, psycho-pedagogues, clinical philosophers, psychiatrists help with self-knowledge, because we often deceive ourselves with a distorted image of ourselves. This image and insufficient knowledge feeds the illusion and hinders the construction of meaning, because dedicating your life to something, knowing what to stick to depends on self-knowledge. Without knowing ourselves, it's difficult to know what to stick to, because self-knowledge gives us a sense of our limits. And this knowledge is essential when it comes to thinking about meaning, since possible freedom is experienced in situations. Situation is how phenomenologists refer to the spaces of my choice, the facticity of age, for example.

Constructing meaning is not a simple mission. It's difficult to make sense of it because it's very personal, others can help, but only we can make sense of our lives. Meaning is our own and requires effort. Meaning needs to be our own work, because only we know our limitations, only we live our pain, only we experience our emptiness, we know what makes us happy and where we want to go. Therefore, the meaning of our personal lives is not found in a cupboard to be picked up, nor is it bought in the supermarket or given to us as a gift, it is made through choices, self-knowledge, responsibility and dedication. It is born out of our dedication. Nor is it something you take possession of like a car or a house. Our lives don't have meaning in the same way as a designer watch. The relationship expressed by the verb to have is different in both cases. One is of possession, I have the watch, the other is of autonomy, I build my destiny.

The Spanish philosopher Ortega y Gasset used to say that life is given to us, but it is not given to us ready-made, meaning that constructing meaning was a continuous task that required commitment. Each person needs to find out what they want to do, but not everyone does it competently. There are those who have built their lives in such a way that they are admirable, because they are full of humanity, of good achievements, of things that give satisfaction and nourish the inner self. These people endure setbacks more easily, are not shaken by inhustics, cope better with inconsistencies, feel rewarded and loved, do not envy, do not gossip, are not easily hurt, and live well with themselves.

Anyone who has not done the task of meaning well is unhappy. And it's not just a matter of not looking for meaning. Often, the search for a false meaning, something that has nothing to do with the person, but which they take on because of someone else's influence, also leads to failure. And look at what accompanies it in these cases: envy, exaggerated egoism, lies, bad moods; the frequent use of compensation, sleeping and waking pills. For this reason, philosophers and psychologists have devoted a great deal of time to addressing the question of meaning and explaining its importance.

The question of meaning arose with the understanding of the philosophers of the last century that life takes place in time, and the construction of the future as an experience of freedom. If we are what we become, the challenge of living seems to be to overcome what prevents us from getting where we hope to be. Man appears, in this understanding, as a being of the future, as a being who is not ready but who is making himself, someone in process.

The German philosopher Martin Heidegger was able to express this understanding systematically. It seems to him that man is a nothingness of being, that is, his being is not determined, but is made. Technically, it is said that man defines himself by being or not being what he is. Ortega y Gasset managed to say this in a familiar way. He said that man doesn't have a nature, he has a history, or that man's nature is to be historical. That's the point, man is a being that changes, nothing is ready. Heidegger describes man's life in three key terms: dereliction, project and fall. By the first, he means that man emerges for no reason, when he is born he has many possibilities, he can go many places. It also means that there is no path mapped out in advance, no plan that he receives ready-made at birth. With the second term, he says that man is heading towards something with which he hopes to give a reason for his life. Without this journey, without this direction, life has no meaning. That is, there is no prior meaning, but man acquires it in the movement towards the future. The notion of falling is curious because it translates a familiar experience. The movement to construct meaning is a launch into the future, but it is a movement without certainty. In other words, you can't be sure of the path you've chosen. You can lose yourself in this movement towards the future. They often do this when they get lost in their daily tasks, when they dedicate themselves only to the day-to-day and stay in the routine without changing what annihilates them. He blends in with the things he encounters in the world and becomes like them.

Many people experience this fall. And it is accompanied by existential anguish, a feeling that expresses our insecurity with what has to be. This anguish arises from the discovery that nothing sustains the construction of meaning apart from what exists. If we get stuck in a routine, if we're busy with the daily grind and don't go beyond it, we lose ourselves. It degrades existence to live for no reason, just to be there until death comes. Every day we die a little and watch people end their lives, young and old, sick and healthy, of natural causes, murdered or in accidents. Death is an everyday reality.

This dramatic reality of falling seems to have become commonplace during the great European wars. Anyone who watches films or reads novels about what was happening in Europe during the years of the great conflicts has the feeling that life is this imminent risk of loss. Life going to nothing, if experienced in this way, is not bearable. The risk, however, that accompanies it is the opportunity to give it meaning. He contemplates this challenge of building meaning by weaving the future, with relationships of love and friendship, replacing that initial nothingness of meaning with something. The result of this process of building meaning is love, art, science, religion and philosophy. In other words, what we do to make sense is concretized in culture. This is what is said in *Man and Philosophy, short meditations on existence and culture.* Acts of culture are expressions of meaning. And they are all the more fulfilling the more the individual gives himself up and puts himself into the work he is doing. In other words, as an objectification of value, in culturalist language (2007, p. 43): "a meditation on man needs to consider that he creates and absorbs culture, but does so according to existential demands,"

After the Great Wars, especially the second, the experience of falling and emptiness did not fundamentally change. On the contrary, even with a more stable and materially secure life, the generations that followed lost themselves in childishness, uncultivation and an inability to deal with their feelings. About this uneducated and unhappy man, the Spanish philosopher Ortega y Gasset says in a 1930 work called *La rebelion de las masas* that he (1994, p. 208): "walks everywhere and no matter where he imposes his intimate barbarism, he is, in effect, the minnow of human history" (p. 208). This mass man is also a satisfied little lord, says Ortega y Gasset, the one who (id., p. 213): "knows that certain things cannot be and yet, and for this very reason, pretends by his own actions and words to the contrary conviction." He is a new barbarian, an expression of today's unculture, because as an expert (id., p. 218): "knows very well about the tiniest place in the universe, but ignores the root of everything else." What's worse, despite his lack of culture, he sets the tone for social life and even pretends to direct it (id., p. 207): "the vulgar man, once directed, has decided to rule the world."

From the perspective of meaning, mass man has not been able to create meaning. He doesn't know what to focus on, he doesn't really dedicate himself to anything. He behaves as if life were already ready, that of society and his own. If he undertakes an activity, the task is far from satisfying. The project is born out of the demands of routine or is offered by someone else in the sense of being someone else's project. Many people carry their parents', grandparents', uncles', friends', etc. projects on their backs, but not their own. In these cases, the person goes through life expecting approval for what they do, they depend on their friends telling them that the clothes they wear are nice, they depend on the flattery of their colleagues to feel valued at work, they depend on others for everything they do. To put it in philosophical language, at the ontological level, you are not the master of your situation, because you don't have your life in your hands.

Then they need the other person's approval. It's not about the legitimate satisfaction of others' recognition of what you do well, which occurs naturally and without deliberate seeking, but about the obsessive and continuous need for the other's approval. Life seems organized, but the person says it's boring, bitter and difficult. Every day they wake up is a new stage of unhappiness, often incomprehensible to them. How many people say they have a wonderful family, a good job, a wonderful husband or wife, a good car, obedient and devoted children, the house of their dreams, etc. and find themselves lost in life. They live sad and suffering, unhappy in anguish and depression. They live with the feeling that their life is being wasted.

It's not hard to see why they have failed to make sense. And this is often not the result of bad will. It is true that many people devote little time to the task of making meaning, but there is a continual risk of failure even for those who do. The construction of meaning is risky. Living involves risks, not because here or there the risk appears. Risk is part of life. Dereliction, the project and the fall sum up the risk of existence. Living is risky because of the insecurity in carrying out the project, as Gilberto Kujawski summarized in *Viver e perigoso* (1986, p. 3): "Life is constitutively danger because to live is to address oneself to the future and this hovers in our path of total uncertainty and insecurity, an eclipse of plenitude or an abyss of annihilation."

When we talk about meaning as an important part of human life, we remember Viktor Frankl. He was a psychologist who gave importance to what occupied people's lives. He went through difficult times. As a Jew, he was imprisoned in a concentration camp during the Second World War. He spent three years in prison. When he was released, he returned to Vienna and found his references destroyed. His father had died in the concentration camp. His mother and brother were killed in the gas chamber at *Auschwitz.* His wife had also been killed at the age of twenty-five in Bergen-Belsen. His friends were dead or missing when the Great War ended and he was released. The life he had built before the war was destroyed. And from these losses he rose again without hurt or resentment to care for the pain of others. He dedicated himself to helping people find meaning in their lives.

He gave admirable meaning to his suffering existence because he was true to himself and to what he understood human life to be. At the end of his life, when he was asked about the meaning of his life, he said that the meaning of his life was to help people find the meaning of their lives. And that's what he did most admirably as a psychotherapist and man of faith: helping people to find a way through the mire of existence.

An observer of the human soul, he was one of the creators of existential psychology or existential analysis applied to psychology. The whole discussion around meaning had a philosophical meaning. Frankl shows that it is also a medical question. His writings have been examined by important names in existential phenomenology such as Karl Jaspers and Ludwig Binswanger. Philosophers such as Gabriel Marcel and Martin Heidegger have also commented on his theses. He became known for having developed a psychotherapeutic technique around the will to meaning. With this concept he called what the existentialists called self-transcendence, which means directing one's life towards something that is beyond and outside. To live by building a relationship like a beloved son, by opening oneself up to the beauty of a beloved woman and to friendship. To live for a mission, to create beauty, to illustrate splendor, to take care of pain and restore patients' health, to speak of God and open one's life to realities beyond the routine. Giving meaning to one's life has to do with what occupies and is unique to the person.

Frankl didn't just see the pain and evil around him. He told of a Catholic woman who risked her life for years by keeping a cousin of his hidden, and that he remembered a lawyer who, for no apparent reason and in times of the greatest deprivation, offered him food whenever he met him. His teacher, circumstantially affiliated with the Nazi party, had helped him at the beginning of the war to protect and save patients diagnosed as schizophrenic from death. And so, by suffering what few people suffer and seeing the efforts of those who struggle to alleviate suffering, he fought the idea of collective guilt as an irreparable harm that each person does to themselves. Even when there is objective responsibility for evil, which can be said of the Germans in their persecution of the Jews, there is no personal guilt. Frankl's lessons seem fundamental because they indicate that man has the final word when it comes to acting. Even in unfavorable circumstances, he can take a different path. We often hear today that the way political disputes are structured in Brazil favors corruption and the practice of evil. And it does seem that way, but this is not an acceptable justification for the perpetuation of corruption. It is at best a regrettable explanation. Man can act ethically.

His feelings, thoughts and actions were at a high level. Envy, resentment and revenge did not reach him there. He assumed a fundamental principle of ethics: guilt is personal, it makes no sense to blame an entire nation. Not all Germans were murderers, not all of them agreed with the monstrosities of Nazism. Frankl saw the evil that was done to him and also the good that was done in such harsh times. He didn't hide the good or stop fighting evil.

In the third lecture of his book *The Question of Meaning in Psychotherapy, Frankl* explained the question of meaning and its importance in people's lives. He examined the behavior of the prisoners in the concentration camp. In their daily work, these suffering and sick men thought exclusively about the bowl of soup offered to them in the evening, when their work routine in the concentration camp ended. They waited for that dish as if it were everything. They didn't have the ordinary worries of people in their normal lives, such as: going to work, paying the bills, taking their children to school. This loss of a singular life and of their own history began with their arrival in the camp. All the prisoner's belongings were taken from him, only his glasses and suspenders remained. Even his hair was shaved. Along with the retained belongings, it was as if his past was also left there, says the author (1990, p. 98): "he takes for granted his entire existence up to the present." Once the phase of eliminating the past has passed, man falls into an undignified existence, especially when he dedicates himself to self-preservation, he loses all the dynamics of inner life. Then he becomes an animal fighting for food, dreaming of a plate of food and, in this fight, mistreating the weakest. He also becomes a herd animal, hiding among the others so as not to be noticed, making an enormous effort to dilute himself in the mass. Being noticed often meant death. Even though this was the most common attitude among prisoners, there were those who did not dehumanize themselves and (1990, p. 100): "instead of regressing, they progressed much more inwardly." Which men managed to maintain their dignity and even rise spiritually in such unfavorable circumstances? Those who had a direction, a support transcendent to life itself (id., p. 101): "This support could exist in two ways: either it was a support in the future, or it was a support in eternity." Hence the practical proof of the importance of meaning, concludes the author (id., p. 103): "recalling the words of Nietzsche, who once uttered the following phrase: whoever has a reason for living, endures almost everything as (...) (as - they are those circumstances of life that made life in the countryside so difficult)."

The last part of this prisoner psychology considers the moment of release. Physical liberation is not everything. Freed from the camp, the ex-prisoner was not happy, he didn't feel things, because he had been intimately destroyed. When he returned to the town where he had lived before the war, the ex-prisoner was hurt by the fact that people either said they didn't know about his situation or that they had also suffered persecution. Maybe everyone was responsible for what happened, but you can be responsible without being guilty, like when I get sick and go to the doctor. Even if I'm not to blame for the illness, I'm responsible for paying the doctor.

The survivors of the camp, when they regained some of their humanity, had one thought that tormented and depressed them: they knew that the best men didn't make it out of the camp alive. They were the first to be noticed and the first to be killed. This is Frankl's fundamental lesson: those who managed to survive had a reason to live, a direction that preserved their dignity and gave them ways to survive those difficult times.

The conclusion of the three lectures is as follows (1990, p. 109): "man in spite of everything - in spite of necessity and death (first lecture), in spite of physical or mental suffering (second lecture), or under the weight of fate in the concentration camp (third lecture) - can say yes to life." Frankl ends the book lightly and calmly, demonstrating the importance of meaning in life as the nourishment of hope.

In addition to this work, Frankl's other book *Man's Search for Meaning* was read in churches and synagogues and became compulsory reading in universities around the world in the middle of the last century. In this book, the author talks about the importance of living for something and that it was only this openness that helped people survive the extermination camp.

The question of meaning has become close to what Ortega y Gasset called the existential project, because it relates to what life expects us to do, which is more than what we think we need to do.

You learn from Frankl's books precious lessons in psychology and philosophy, you learn from his example how to stand up when life seems to have taken everything away from you. The construction of meaning is a task of continuous recycling, because meaning is never completely ready. Searching helps us to move in a certain direction.

The question of meaning is broad and does not stop at the intellectual dimension. Every choice has an inevitable individual character and a rational dimension, but it is not limited to the intellectual, nor does it stop at the phenomenal. The choice is not based on what appears to me at each moment as a perceived reality. We need something that takes us beyond what comes to us, that moves us beyond perceived reality.

As far as the concentration camp men mentioned by Frankl in his books are concerned, those who managed to endure very difficult living conditions survived because they believed in the impossible and sought it out. Whether that impossibility was returning home, to the hot coffee table, the warm cake, the soft bed and the delight of sleeping in clean sheets after a hot bath and the company of loved ones; or the hope in a God capable of inspiring love in suffering, confidence in resurrection and the certainty that in the end, in the midst of the world's misery, justice and goodness will prevail. The idea of meaning can also be found in a supernatural faith, depending on the individual.

Self-understanding is the basis of choice, alongside faith and hope. The construction of a meaning capable of making life seem good requires us to know ourselves. It requires us to be able to bear and carry through the choices we make. It requires surrender. In other words, meaning demands giving, it demands love, and they will only come if we know who we are and how much the chosen route will warm our hearts. Only when we know ourselves well can we make every act the construction of a meaning that satisfies us. Without this, the journey through life will seem unimportant.

Therefore, without the hope that comes from believing in the future, without the surrender that comes from love, without the self-knowledge that shows what we are and what we are capable of, meaning will not be built. Making someone the creator of their own life is one of the most important tasks; meaning is the ultimate reason for human learning.

The question of meaning therefore goes back to faith and belief in what moves us. And that's what we'll talk about next, what sustains us in existence, even in the moments of greatest adversity.

6 Believing in the reasonable

The discovery of subjectivity was one of the great achievements of modern man. Its expression in thought was the result of the intellectual movements that began in the Renaissance and continued into the early modern period. The certainty sustained in subjective consciousness seemed to come from rationality, it just seemed that way. This is what Ortega y Gasset observed in the eighth lesson of his book *Que es Filosofia?* There he examined modern subjectivity and referred to it thus:

> In me, of course, the most varied landscapes appear; everything that I naively believed I had around me and that I believed to be there and to support me, is now reborn as inner fauna and flora. These are states of my subjectivity. To see is not to leave oneself, but to find in oneself the image of this theater, a piece of the image of the universe. Consciousness is always with me, it is tenant and dwelling at the same time, it is intimacy - the superlative and fundamental intimacy of myself with myself (ORTEGA Y GASSET, 1997, p. 377).

Ortega's description affirms what he suggested denying: the certainty that seems to come from rational justifications depends on beliefs that are beyond those justifications. Certainty comes from belief; convictions are anchored in them. It is in intimate persuasion that thoughts articulated by reason are sustained. And human life only gains the strength it can have when it is an expression of faith and when rationality does not contradict beliefs. What moves us in existence is faith, although not an irrational faith.

It's not hard to see that this is the case with us. What happened to the man of the last century when he was told that the universe was not infinite, but finite, albeit very large and expanding? People changed what they thought about the universe, but they continued to believe in science and its ability to offer truths about the world. For people with the beliefs of modernity, that's all there is to it, as long as there is no doubt about the credibility of science and the information it provides. However, what happens if we lose confidence in something that is crucial to us, if we lose, for example, hope in the future, confidence in a dear friend or loved one? Our personal lives plunge into chaos and remain there until we re-establish new beliefs that allow us to live. When we lose trust in someone, we become disappointed and angry. It seems that building a new belief is the foundation of a new meaning.

Belief is the starting point for future choices. In paragraph 30 of *La idea de principio en Leibniz y la evolucion de la teoria deductiva, Ortega y Gasset* wrote:

> It is shameful that there is no essential description of the form that life takes when it exists on the basis of beliefs, just as it has not persuasively recounted the most important, most serious event that can occur in history and that has often occurred: the loss or disappearance of a belief, that strange and dramatic peripeteia in which a large group goes from believing wholeheartedly in a figure in the world to doubting it (ORTEGA Y GASSET, 1994, p. 286).

Which belief is the philosopher talking about? Is there more than one type of belief?

Every belief has irrational components, but the beliefs that move people need to be acceptable, they can't go against reason. Beliefs that don't pass the sieve of rationality can therefore be rejected. We accept a belief that doesn't lose the reference of reason, but which points in the direction of what lies beyond the perceptions of phenomena and which can give it density, anchoring known truths. And when we think, we are either under the rigor of a restricted method, as occurs in science, or we come across something that is beyond what is shown in consciousness, when we place ourselves in the philosophical perspective. In any case, there is always a lot to say and think about when we use reason properly. It tells us very little and our perceptual experience of the world even less.

Hasn't the development of modern reason invalidated many beliefs? Haven't we learned that beliefs are unfounded thoughts? Hasn't the development of science allowed us to overcome erroneous beliefs held for centuries? Didn't the Enlightenment, as a cultural movement of philosophy, help to leave behind the untrue acceptance of something as truth? The answer to all these questions is positive, but the proper use of reason and the recognition of the truths of science have only eliminated beliefs that are contrary to reason. Karl Jaspers comments on what the use of good reason has enabled us to overcome and refers to what remains subject to reason. Jaspers called the misuse of reason against reasonable beliefs a false enlightenment. He says so in *Scientific Initiation:*

> False enlightenment thinks it can base all knowledge, will and action on simple understanding, instead of using understanding only as an indispensable way of clarifying what has to be provided; it absolutizes the always particular knowledge of understanding instead of sensibly applying it to the domain that belongs to it. (False enlightenment) in short, wants man to be self-sufficient in such a way that he achieves all that is true and essential through his understanding. He just wants to know and not believe. True enlightenment, on the other hand, although it does not impose a limit on thought and the possibility of questioning from outside and by coercion, is nevertheless aware of the factual limit. Because not only does it want to clarify what has not yet been investigated, prejudices and supposed evidence, but it also clarifies itself. It does not confuse the paths of understanding with the contents of the human being. The latter appear as susceptible to clarification through rational understanding, but not susceptible to substantiation in the understanding itself (JASPERS, 1987, p. 82/83).

Jaspers' text is enlightening, as it consolidates the truths of science and philosophy, preserves the importance of reason, but points out its limits by taking up that precious lesson from Emmanuel Kant: reason needs to be aware of its limits. And so, the proper use of reason manages to make it clear that there is no way to remove all beliefs from life.

On the other hand, confidence in reason open to reasonable beliefs comes with the overcoming of Comtean positivism, which reduced reason to its experimental dimension and philosophy to a synthesis of the sciences. This limited way of thinking entered the philosophical tradition as positivism and included among the laws of history the belief in effortless progress and fed the false belief in a future closed to transcendence. Positivism was conceived by a scientific civilization, but it was far removed from confidence in man's ability and in the logic of life. A reasonable belief is not frozen in dogma, much less in the laws of a limiting and limited science. For this reason, a life based on good beliefs means overcoming philosophical positivism.

Ortega y Gasset deepens this understanding and argues in paragraph 26 of *La idea de principle en Leibniz y la evolucion de la teoria deductiva* that intellectual truths are based on beliefs. Ortega says that every philosophical construction is based on beliefs, without which the theories constructed would fall like a house of cards. And he goes further by saying that belief is what sustains the philosopher when he thinks, because everything he creates depends on the (1994, p. 259): "living reality of the beliefs where he is, in which he is, lives and moves, like the Christians in Christ, according to St. Paul."

What can we make of these references? That the life we have only accomplishes all it can when it moves, with some awareness, on beliefs. Belief is the starting point of our life, best when the belief is not hidden and is conscious of its presence at the base of thought. Beliefs enable us to accomplish great things, as Jesus said in Matthew's gospel (Mt 17:21-22): "Because of your little faith," he said, "I tell you the truth, if you have faith as a grain of mustard seed, I will say to that mountain, 'Move from here to there,' and it will move; and nothing will be impossible for you." It's clear that Jesus wasn't talking about changing the laws of the world, the work of the Father, but about changing the world in which we move. The final phrase stands out: nothing is impossible for those who believe and give themselves over to this faith.

This faith that keeps us in existence is the same faith that brings about great achievements. And it will only be so if it is a whole, complete, unquestionable faith. When we talk about faith, it's inevitable to bring up the question of religion. Belief in God is not supported by reason, but the proper exercise of reason opens the way to God. Faith in God, if we work with the presuppositions presented here, is the same faith in life, in the future and in man that we find in Matthew's Gospel (Mt 6:25): "For all things I say to you, do not worry about your life, what you will eat or drink, or about your body, what you will wear. Is not the body more than clothing, and life more than food?"

The fundamental thing about absolute trust in life is that it doesn't mean carelessness or laziness. Jesus' words don't mean that we can stop working or that we don't have to make an effort to meet our needs. If we want bread, we need to prepare the soil, plant it, water it, watch the grain grow, harvest it and then prepare it for the oven. After all this process, the bread arrives at our table: fragrant, tasty and nutritious. The work, the planning, the effort are not at issue in Jesus' words, but the confidence in the result of the effort, planning and dedication, the belief and hope that the commitment and dedication will bring the expected result. It is against the anguish of distrust, and against the lack of faith in the future that Jesus speaks, because if we follow the laws that the Creator has made, the reward will come. His words indicate that faith in God is no different from faith in man and in the future. They converge on responsibility for our lives. Faith in man and in God cannot do without effort and intelligence, but both point to the belief that the future has guarantees beyond human effort. The immediate future may not be what we dream of, but insistence on what is right will take us in the desired direction.

This confidence in the future, based on effort and intelligence, on the achievements of science, technology and reason, is what the modern world has bequeathed to our time. What we have been given is confidence in a future made of man's efforts, a future that will not have automatic results. And if we put aside the blind faith in the progress of history, which was a perversion of the 19th century, we will once again find hope in the future to be built. A future that depends on man, that won't happen automatically, but finds hope in belief in the effort made.

Recalling Jesus' words about the power of belief, it seems necessary to place it in the space of human respect and love. In other words, there will be no future, no hope, if there is no care for people and the world we need to live in. There will be no future in a world where injustice, inequality and evil grow. In other words, there will be no hope in a society made out of the morality of which Kant spoke, because it is only as a moral creation that a society rises above nature and animal instinct to make something new. Confidence in life requires a moral commitment to change the way we live. A moral world described by Kant in the imperatives of reason, but which is already announced in the books of the New Testament (Rev. 21:6): "He who sat on the throne said: I renew all things."

The great utopias of the West originated or were at least inspired by the renewal represented by the message of Jesus. Examples include the society of the Holy Spirit of the monk Joaquim de Fiori, the society of Thomas Munzer and even the city of Canudos created by Antonio Conselheiro. In all these proposals for social life there is the confidence that the future of mankind is not far from the Kingdom of God. Of course, this Kingdom is an ideal, a model, not something ready-made, although its elements can be foreseen.

In short, it is beliefs that ensure life and the feeling of security that allows us to go into the future.

7 Touching God's problem

We've said before that what moves people through life is what they believe. That's why we often find ways to move on when there seems to be no reason to do so, start a relationship again after huge disappointments and the promise of no new love, rethink life and start a new stage every time we feel we're not happy with ourselves and believe the promises made to us. Beliefs take us forward in life, they keep us on our feet and because of what they mean, they acquire great importance in our lives. It is these beliefs that guide us every time we start a new life cycle, every time we start something again. And so we have to ask ourselves: what is a cycle?

It has already been said that a cycle is a period of time consisting of a certain number of years in which the world returns to its beginning. This notion of a cosmic cycle was conceived by the Greek Anaximander and Pythagorean philosophers as a valid way of dealing with change. It became common among the ancient Greeks. It was inspired by the cycles of nature: the seasons, day and night, etc. In modern thought, this idea of the cycle reappeared in Nietzsche, for whom the eternal return is the reaffirmation of the world. Oswald Splenger also used the notion of the temporal cycle to explain the evolution of societies, which he compared to the development of an organism. For him, every society was born at one time, developed, reached fullness and then went into decline. These conclusions enshrined in philosophical tradition have in common the attempt to describe a phenomenon that repeats itself according to a pattern. We don't consider this to be the best way to look at time. It seems more reasonable to look at it from a linear perspective, although without talking about rigid patterns of change. And what does the notion of a cycle aim to solve? The existence of common elements in a period of time, whether for a society or an individual. A cycle is a specific period, with well-defined and coherent elements in a timeline. A cycle in personal life is the years of being single, the time spent married, starting over after years in a particular job or profession. A cultural cycle is a set of intellectual, aesthetic, technical, religious aspects and beliefs that typify an era. In short, we see a cycle as an expression of a time in which various aspects of life are well defined and linked to each other. When a cycle is completed, we see a new period emerge with other characteristics, beliefs and theories.

In each cycle, whether personal or cultural, we see the predominance of beliefs and theories. In cultural terms, cycles look like periods in which certain beliefs remain. Beliefs characterize great moments in history, as Ortega y Gasset taught. This is why explanations survive for long periods without being questioned, because they have strong beliefs underneath their reasoning. It also explains what happens when the beliefs collapse, the reasoning behind them is questioned and the whole set collapses. So says Ortega *in La idea de principle en Leibniz y la evolution de la teoria deductiva:*

> It is not known that what is most alive in ideas is not what is clearly in the forefront of our minds when we think of them, but what has been thought underneath them, what remains underground when we use them. These invisible, hidden ingredients are sometimes the millennia-old experiences of a people. This latent depth of ideas, which sustains, occupies and nourishes them, cannot be transferred, like anything that is truly human (ORTEGA Y GASSET, 1994, p. 215).

Belief seems fundamental because when faced with questions about why we live, about the meaning of our suffering, limitations and weaknesses, about the reason for our pain, disappointment and anguish, we can't find a strong enough reason in reason or in our experience of the world. If we stick to the facts of the world, everything that happens seems meaningless. The answer to such important questions is hidden in a veil of mystery and this is the space of beliefs. What reasoning does is put ideas under suspicion and then, if the beliefs are absurd, they will reveal their fragility.

Among the many beliefs that touch us, perhaps the belief in God is the one that most mobilizes human consciousness and the one that has gained projection the most times in the history of man. Treating belief in God separately does not mean that it is unreasonable, while others are, or at least seemed to be for a long time. What happens when belief leads to irrationality? It promotes disaster because if there are no clear reasons for so many essential things and questions, when irrationality feeds belief it leads to absurdities and atrocities.

There are many examples of irrationality. Belief in the superiority of one group has led to terrible actions in the last century. This is what happened in Nazi Germany with the mass extermination of the Jews. There is also the belief in the superiority of the belief and the justification for its imposition. When we critically analyze the crusades in the Middle Ages, the prototype for other religious wars, we realize the inappropriateness of violence practiced in the name of God. Few things mobilize us more than belief in God. For this reason, Karl Jaspers wrote in the chapter on Man in his *Philosophical Beginnings* that it is the judgment and experience of God gleaned from tradition that must guide our faith:

> Through transcendence we are guided differently than any other guide in the world, because there is only one way to be guided by God. This is the way to freedom itself. God's voice is in everything that comes to an individual with a certain character, when they are open to what they encounter in tradition and in the world around them. Man is guided by his judgment of his own actions. It is this judgment that inhibits or impels him, corrects or confirms him. The voice of God judging human actions has only one temporal expression, which is man's judgment of his feelings, motivations and actions (JASPERS, 1987, p. 63).

Jaspers' reference to the experience of God and the role that critical meditation plays in purifying this belief are fundamental in the text quoted. Since belief moves us, an unmeditated belief can lead to actions that go against what we believe, and this risk increases in an age of mysticism and fundamentalism. Time and time again, we have seen examples of terrorist attacks that surpass each other in brutality and irrationality. The attack on the twin towers in New York in 2001, the attacks on the London Underground and Paris in 2015 are examples of this. The justification, however absurd it may seem, is the belief in God and the right to kill and torture the infidel. The absurdity of the fact is that religions preach peace and not violence, and only an ill-considered belief can lead to such a conclusion.

When we mention mysticism as an experience that disregards rational criticism, we don't mean all the mystics of the Christian tradition. There are those like St. Bonaventure who did not deny the importance of reasoning, but we are referring to the basic attitude disseminated by Neoplatonism. Plotinus understood that God could not be reached through rationality or any human ability and suggested ecstasy as a way of meeting the divine. He believed that in this way man would reach the intimacy of God. In general, the so-called Christian mystics have little dialogue with rationality, as in the case of Joan of Arc. It is also important to note that not every mystical experience, even those that are not based on rationality, move towards irrationality, brutality and ignorance. In general, this is not the case, but there are risks and they are greater the further mystics move away from theological studies.

Religious fundamentalism is proving to be more dangerous than mysticism. This is because a literal interpretation of the sacred texts of any religion often leads to the opposite of what the doctrine as a whole intends to communicate. The sacred texts are ancient, they were written in a different context to ours and to communicate the faith to a people with different problems and perspectives to our own. What's more, they were written with no other concern than catechesis, without journalistic care, without the accuracy and/or objectivity of a historical account. To take these texts literally, even more so with the hermeneutic resources we have at our disposal today, is to risk taking positions and doing things that are not backed up by a reflected experience of God. Ill-considered beliefs lead to absurdities and they can be avoided with the knowledge we have today to purify the experience of God. That's what we need to do, submit the reported experience of other times to a careful reflection of the sacred texts, with the humility of knowing that we can make mistakes in this interpretation. At best, we will arrive at an approximate understanding of the teaching, but that is better than complete ignorance.

The experience of God is limited because our understanding of freedom and love is approximate. It is limited because it is conditioned by the human reality it possesses: a material dimension that binds us to time and space, a life limited by fragile biological processes, a psychological consciousness with suffering and a spirit limited by the capacity to know. God does not live according to our finitude. Recognizing human limitations in the face of God's infinite freedom and love does not prevent us from accepting God, even if we can only have a limited experience of him. However, our limited experience of love and freedom, which places us above things, is the place we have for meeting God. It is not a place of refusal, because the freedom I experience is not annihilated by the freedom of the other, that is, the freedom of the other does not have to be annihilated for me to be free. On the contrary, the freedom of each of us is qualified by the freedom of the people who pass through our lives. Only in the face of other freedom does my freedom become attentive to things that I wouldn't consider if I were dealing with things without freedom. When I choose a shirt from my wardrobe, my freedom doesn't have to consider anything other than the circumstances in which I'm going to wear it. When I choose someone as a friend, their freedom requires that my choices be made carefully from then on. The same goes for someone I take to be my beloved. The other person's freedom demands that I be careful how I conduct my love and my choices, because my freedom can kill love. Both love and freedom need to be worked on every day. In the face of the other's love and freedom, my love and freedom are not annihilated, they are demanded.

Jean Paul Sartre comments that the experience of God is not justified because it expresses bad faith. His argument is based on the fact that it is an essential part of human life to experience security, peace and happiness alongside frustration and the fear of finitude. To fail to consider the second part of human reality is to lose oneself as a man, because the two experiences come together. The bad faith stems from the fact that, unable to experience his own limitations and finitudes without falling into boredom, man finds no meaning in life and creates a consolation. Thus, Sartre's God wants to occupy the place that the ancient Greeks attributed to the Metaphysical Being, and since it is not possible to have an objective view of this Being, man is unable to experience it. The great problem of the metaphysics that took place among the Greeks was precisely to identify in the provisional the definitive that justified it.

The experience of God, however, does not cancel out man's limited and finite reality. It shows that we are in the presence of an unreachable Being. Man becomes aware that everything he talks about must become the object of his consciousness and as such cannot be absolutized. That is to say, God is not experienced from the relative, but is only present as a possibility that arises beyond the phenomenal. God is greater than what I think of him or what I am. Therefore, God is not something that can be objectified or compared with the things of the world. The Christian faith teaches that everything that exists cannot be compared to God, although his Kingdom is announced as near, he himself dwells in a place far from us. And the argument of bad faith seems to fall apart if we admit that our commitment and life is made at the limit of facticity. If we consider the phenomenal reality of man, he cannot be divinized. The experience of and belief in God will only be legitimate if it doesn't eliminate the contradictions of human life and if it doesn't take away man's responsibility to choose his future.

8 Working and changing the world

Work, understood as a planned effort to overcome the difficulties of survival and transform the world into a space more suited to one's needs, is a properly human activity. To live is to act and work is an important form of action. Some animals work, but they do so either under human command or by reproducing instinctive behavioral patterns. Precisely because it involves changing the natural world to make it more in line with our needs, human work has something poetic, aesthetic and creative about it. To the extent that it is part of the construction of meaning, it aims to produce wealth and make existence more beautiful and enjoyable. Work is part of human life, although living is not just about working, as was thought in the 19th century. In that century, European intellectuals emphasized the economic dimension of life. But living is more than working. Work understood in the broad sense of changing reality so that it produces goods and quality of life.

In fact, when we consider human labor from a global perspective and think about what the world would be like without it, we can appreciate its importance. Work prepares fields for planting and fills them with produce, builds wonderful bridges that connect the banks of rivers, lakes and bays, produces many useful things, renews and beautifies the natural landscape. The natural landscape has its charms, but the human landscape, the result of well-planned and executed work, has admirable results in beautifying and enriching society. When we contemplate the flowers in a garden, a beautiful house, monuments such as the Eiffel Tower, the Tower of Pisa, Christ the Redeemer in Rio de Janeiro, the Statue of Liberty at the entrance to New York, when we see the frenetic movement of a port receiving and sending goods, we can't help but admire the transformative power of human work.

It can be said that human life truly began when man started working, although historians take the written record of human activities as the moment in time when history began, leaving the period before writing, known as prehistory, to one side. However, in the mysterious prehistory, when we plunge only into the darkness of the unwritten, it is necessary to separate the period when man only collected, hunted and fled from predators, from when he began to deliberately modify reality: to plant, to organize into groups, to divide tasks, to build dwellings, to make weapons and tools, etc. Work changed the human way of life and made existence a singular reality. The division of labour allowed human society to begin to organize itself.

Work is important to individuals and peoples because of the results it brings. This result distinguishes national groups and separates those who achieve greater productivity from others who fail to get rich. Those who master more advanced technology, have greater knowledge of the production network, dedicate themselves to the activity in a more organized way, achieve superior results. Work produces greater and better results when it is carried out with good technique, when processes are controlled. Personal effort, dedication to the job and group discipline are key elements. However, in today's globalized world, it cannot be said that entire national groups do not dedicate themselves to their work with commitment and therefore fail to overcome their backwardness. There is much more involved in the process of enriching national groups, including the way they insert themselves into the global value chain. If there was a time when personal effort and discipline made a difference in the way people organized their lives, today it seems that this factor is not so significant. What makes the difference between national societies is the quality of the work done, the dominance of high technology, the savings accumulated over generations that allow for more productive investments, the higher pay for educated labor. These factors are more significant than the time dedicated to it and the effort of the group. This is why the most developed countries become even richer, while other nations remain underdeveloped, despite the efforts of their members.

In countries like Brazil, the population generally works long hours and makes an effort. And there's no denying that when we look at the results of decades of effort, we see some progress. If the progress isn't as great, it's due to the low level of education of the workers, the lack of resources for investment, the high interest rate for financing production, etc. and not exactly to a lack of commitment. It's not that commitment isn't fundamental, it is. It's not that greater effort doesn't explain equally greater and better production. It just doesn't explain everything, nor does it justify the level of poverty in some regions of the country. Far from the theory of the exploitation of the rich by the poor, what we are pointing out is that historical and cultural aspects explain the development trajectory of nations and their rate of growth.

In an increasingly globalized world, production chains are interconnected in countries with different levels of development. It is possible to find areas within a country with different levels of development that benefit more than others due to their greater and better integration into the production relations of the world economy. Regions of Brazil such as greater Sao Paulo benefit more from the economic relations established in the global economy than other regions of Brazil. And the people are the same, they work just as hard. And there is a new element in this. The manufacture of global products shows that products made anywhere in the world have quality and are distributed and desired all over the planet. Many of the products of the American industry are designed there, but they have raw materials from anywhere and are produced everywhere. And when it comes to the quality and talent of the best-prepared worker, there is no difference between the Brazilian, Indian or Russian and the workers of the richest nations. For example, the Brazilian dentists who work in Europe with enormous success and quality, or the Russian scientists who, after the end of the Soviet Union, were employed in universities around the world. Today, therefore, there are factors that better explain the difference in development between peoples than simply their dedication to work, although the value attached to work is not negligible.

And if production chains become global, the work of the groups or part of it is worth its weight in the global market. Economic integration values the procedures that are integrated into the production process. Products also gain universal recognition, a similar standard of quality, but not all processes in the global value network command the same remuneration. A car produced anywhere in the world usually has components from various parts of the planet and once it is ready, it will be used everywhere too. This car needs to be as good in New York, Paris, Rome or in the interior of Africa and Latin America. There is no way to produce different things. Therefore, even if the production chains are integrated, this doesn't mean that all stages of the process are paid the same.

In this world where the production process is integrated and where work has the characteristic of being collective, man working in isolation feels alone. And his loneliness expresses individualism, which is different from the singularity that sets us apart, because you can be unique and different, doing what makes you particular without falling into the loneliness of individualism. Individualism is a personal phenomenon, but it has repercussions on society. This time of the masses is paradoxically the time when individualism grows and where it leads to loneliness. The problem of our time is not that people are singular and unique, but that we don't relate to each other properly. And here we're not talking about the quantity of relationships, but the quality. In this time of the masses, social networks add friends in large numbers. However, a friend can't be added at the touch of a computer or phone screen, it takes a long time of living together, building trust and sharing a story. To have a friend you need to create bonds, to captivate the heart, as the little prince in Antoine Saint-Exupery's story said, but this is not the case. In other words, the globalized world of work not only strengthens individualism, it reinforces loneliness.

A worker who assembles a car with a French engine, electronic equipment from the United States, tires from Indonesia, headlights from Argentina, is still only on the assembly line. His reality as an assembler is no different from the workers of the last century, only the production process is more integrated. He remains distanced from other men. As a person, his work remains isolated and he doesn't see himself as an agent of history. He remains in superficial relationships, without a meaning that transcends his productive routine, without feeding his soul, without building a greater meaning for life. If this activity doesn't delight him, and it often doesn't, he will sink into boredom and indifference, if not sadness or depression. And he is in a worse situation when he is not integrated into the world production process, because without participating in the creation of world products, he will be paid less. Then the unhappiness, boredom and depression will be compounded by a lack of reasonable options. This man will have few options in life, his choices will be very limited, although they will never be completely eliminated.

Dissatisfaction results from superficial relationships, little awareness of the results of work and low pay. This is how the workers of the world are. Some will be a little poorer and have a worse life, but all are lonely and sad. The way forward for humanity in the world of work is through better salaries, but to be well you need much more. Man needs to find a greater reason for his work so that he doesn't fall into the slavery of routine; he needs to create creative spaces between the activities that he doesn't see as important. And this is a personal task: you can't create meaning in life unless you do it personally. We are talking about a path of personal elevation that goes beyond daily work, a capacity to understand the world and its processes that is not limited to technical learning either. It means setting out on a path of personal growth that combines the creation of meaning with the experience of the beautiful and the poetic. This is what a good humanistic education can offer.

Lost in the midst of low-quality cultural production broadcast on the open media, workers in different countries are unlikely to come into contact with quality cultural production. They are unlikely to have moments of meditation, to be enthusiastic about good reading or the aesthetic enjoyment of works of art. Without this openness to the beautiful, the intelligent and the good, they will be lost in routine and in a world of work poor in opportunities.

However, despite the weight of routine and the low level of education of workers in the less developed world, and the appeals of consumerism in the rich world, there are reasons for hope when workers manage to go beyond basic needs and look for a job that fulfills them, a job in which they feel responsible for the future of society and their own destiny. It is this work that brings him closer to personal meaning, which brings him closer to his best possibilities and saves him from meaningless consumerism, boring routine and sadness. Because having goods to live is important, but living is not about accumulating goods that have nothing to do with the personal meaning of life. And when we see that mechanical or repetitive work increasingly requires elements of quality that demand intellectual preparation, we also find reasons for hope in this. In our time, it is no longer possible to separate manual and intellectual work, because almost nothing nowadays is one or the other in isolation. All work carried out with today's technology is part intellectual and part manual.

By pointing out these reasons for hope, it is clear that the global production system is not concerned with offering more creative work, much less integrating all workers into the global production process or distributing wealth more equitably. The owners of capital, often thousands of people represented by any one company, are only looking to enrich themselves, but leave interesting loopholes in the system. The ecological concern linked to human survival is one of them, somehow it has become a common concern. It is possible to insert yourself into the global value chain, with some creativity, with personal elements in the production process, it is also possible to seek levels of cultural training beyond technical learning and, above all, to seek personal, intellectual, critical growth and self-knowledge. All this knowledge and skills is not completely linked to the world of work, but it is related to it. This creative process of spiritual formation includes elements that go beyond the world of work, but finds possibilities for development in it.

Only when nourished by these creative elements will work with today's characteristics point towards a more human life, a life of building meaning, self-knowledge and good fulfillment. Although this is not the purpose of big business or the capital that feeds the world's stock exchanges, these goals can be achieved because the man of our time, especially in the richest nations, wants more than simply to find a job to survive. He hopes to find elements of fulfillment in his work. Although this reality is more visible in more developed nations, these elements are also beginning to emerge in less developed societies, because in a global world, desires are also universalized, not just products.

There is no way of ensuring that the economy of the globalized world will produce anything other than the enrichment of investors, or indirectly promote human progress, but human aspirations are increasingly real in this world. And although today's man still has the characteristics of massification pointed out by Ortega y Gasset in *La rebelion de las masas,* the strengthening of the so-called third sector, the expansion of university education, concern for human rights and dignity, care for ecology are important elements that permeate the world of work and bring opportunities for personal development.

Ortega described mass man as an uncivilized barbarian, said that he didn't meditate on the problems he faced, explained that he knows a lot about almost nothing and that, like a rebellious child, he wants what he knows he can't have. The worker of the globalized world is not very different from this description, except that his technical knowledge is limited to the world of work and he attends little university. He is more individualistic, anxious and hedonistic than Ortega's mass man. However, as has been said, this worker, also the best qualified, is developing a relationship with work that he didn't have before.

The gaps opened up in the world of work will allow these people to discover elements of meaning and cultivate higher quality cultural training. Therein lies the hope of a better life, now that workers all over the world are getting closer to having a more similar life by participating together in the global production process. This is not to say that all workers will follow this path, but it is possible to find a meaning to life that resignifies the whole world of work, if the spaces in the world of work serve as opportunities for meaning.

9 Freeing yourself from circumstance

Going through life, building meaning, is also a way of freeing yourself from threats, or rather, it's an experience of freedom. To live is to choose what we can be in a given circumstance, as Ortega y Gasset said. And our experience of freedom is never absolute. Freedom is getting rid of what life has brought us as a legacy that prevents us from moving forward. While we live, we don't make choices out of thin air; we've been given a lot and it comes along with who we are. If we go to the street to play, it's because we live nearby, if we play with the children in the street it's because they live nearby or have close relatives, if we communicate in a language it's because the society where we were born speaks it, if we adopt a moral code it's because our society uses it, etc.

Those who knew Artur Coimbra as a boy said that he was short and lived in the suburbs of Rio de Janeiro. With that physique, he would hardly have been a top-level athlete. During his youth, he underwent a well-conducted physical training program and, at the beginning of his adult life, he acquired an athlete's body. From then on, after overcoming that initial limitation and training exhaustively, he had a brilliant career as a footballer. Zico, as he became known to fans, freed himself from what prevented him from being a professional footballer. And he was a brilliant player. He could have moaned about his lack of luck in being born a small, poor boy, he could have dedicated himself to other things, but he overcame what was stopping him from doing what he wanted to do, play soccer. Sometimes overcoming doesn't mean changing, but adjusting to what you are. One example is another remarkable athlete who became known as Garrincha. He also became a notable soccer player with crooked legs that would hardly have suited a soccer athlete. However, with his crooked legs he developed an unusual swagger that made him very difficult to mark. And he was a huge success as a player for Botafogo and the Brazilian national team. So, either by changing what is unsuitable for our purposes, or by adjusting what is unsuitable, breaking free is overcoming what prevents us from moving forward. Sometimes the story of liberation from circumstances goes well, sometimes not so well.

Zico and Garrinha are examples of people who knew how to change their circumstances in order to achieve their goals. They realized a life project. And this change from the past depends on the talent of the individual and many things that happen to them, but there are limits to change. Both players haven't stopped belonging to the families they came from. They didn't leave behind their humble origins and many other things couldn't be changed. Many of Garrincha's personal habits led him to an old age in poverty. Philosophers call such things facticity. The key, therefore, to living a project is not to change everything, because that's not possible. What is needed to make a project vital is to change what prevents us from living it or realizing our most important dreams. There is no doubt that many things hinder and prevent change and require us to incorporate them into the project, and many of our dreams will not come true. The freedom experienced in the project is limited, but it shows that human existence does not have a future determined by the past.

Breaking free is a difficult task and often a losing battle. I remember a man who spent his life working hard in a small bakery he had inherited from his father. He had a long routine of hard work, from dawn when he started making the bread until late when he returned home. The months and years passed, his hair bleached, his face filled with wrinkles, his body bent from the effort and scarred by badly healed fractures. He became bitter about the life he inherited and never knew if he wanted. It also seems that he did nothing to change. He saw his wife die of typhoid and his young son take the plunge into drink and drugs. He couldn't overcome his challenges, he couldn't requalify his dreams. He died a failure and unhappy. On the few occasions when I was able to hear him while he was buying sweets or bread, he revealed a bit of bitterness, unhappy with the fate of his family, with the results of his work, with the direction of America do Rio, his team of heart. This man was lost in circumstance and his choices were unable to place him on a satisfactory existential level. He attributed his failures to a lack of opportunity, the death of his wife and the ingratitude of his son. Perhaps he was right, but all of this tied him down in such a way that he was unable to free himself.

The experience of freedom is not absolute. You can't do everything you want. The realization of your life project will have to be based on who you are, the inheritances you have received and the limitations you have. There are things you can't change, like Garrincha's crooked legs or his humble family background. And then there's the relationship with other men, who are also free. And we live among freedoms that somehow influence the choices we make. I can't force another person to love me, admire me or be my friend. Furthermore, personal consciousness has to deal with elements that are part of strata other than thought. The "I" has to live with the weaknesses of the body that cannot be modified, it has to cope with what happens to us, such as the unexpected death of a beloved woman, or it has to overcome the limitations of family poverty. What all these situations have in common is a thickening of reality that means restrictions on freedom. And they do exist. If we can't overcome them, Ortega y Gasset said, they make us lose ourselves, if I don't save myself, or change myself, the circumstance doesn't save me.

Each man will follow his own path, there is no formula that is the same for everyone. It wouldn't work. Building the future in freedom is the task of each person and depends on their uniqueness. The meaning will often need to be renewed or readjusted. This is because a project is not something that can be bought, or that is ready for life. It needs to be adjusted to the facts and what happens to us. Someone who does everything they can to be an athlete and is succeeding in their project could suffer a serious accident and need to readjust their project. As Roger Garaudy says in *Word of Man* (1975, p. 52): "to say that life already has meaning is to misstate the problem. Like having a house or a bank account." What happens is that the project is not a hard, heavy thing, a definitive achievement like a house or an account. It's more like the faint line on the horizon that gives you a sense of direction, but changes as you go. It's true that the house can fall down and the bank can go bankrupt, but things seem like more solid achievements. The project doesn't, it needs to be readjusted if the situation changes and life changes. The project will almost always have to be redone.

Man's life is an experience of freedom. It's not that some things happen to us and therefore the future can't change. A car accident can explain a broken leg, a trip to a malaria region can explain why you contracted the disease. The past explains some things. But if it determines how the bakery inherited in the story told earlier came to be, then no freedom is possible. Man's life cannot be trapped in the past. It is transcendence in time, i.e. going beyond the conditioning that binds us; it is also transcendence towards the other, which occurs when we go beyond the limits of our corporeality.

The experience of transcendence we're talking about is a reaching into the future or an opening up to the other. It's a simple experience that we all have. Transcendence towards the future is what happens when I immerse myself in intense physical training because I hope to be a top athlete, or dedicate myself to the study of psychology when I enter university because I already see myself in clinical practice, for example. Transcending to the other is going to them, to their way of seeing things and perceiving the world, which is different from mine. And then I am able to understand him, I understand his pains and his joys that are not mine. When I go to him, I inhabit his world, at least in part.

The experience of freedom through transcendence is a search for something temporal, but which demands going beyond it, for something that presents itself as the foundation of all beings without identifying itself perfectly with any one entity. When transcendence takes on this dynamic, we enter the universe of philosophy. In this sense, philosophy is an experience of freedom because it takes time beyond time and phenomena beyond them. However, let's stick to the question of existential freedom and the meaning of things without getting into the problems of Metaphysics or Ontology.

The experience of freedom and the construction of meaning. In getting on with life, in choosing to remain a baker or to become a footballer, everyone means things. The footballer does it, the baker does it, we all do it. Without this process of knowing the world, things themselves wouldn't exist, because they only appear in consciousness. And the consciousness that knows the world is also personal and cultural, it identifies what is happening to it and differentiates it from the trajectory of things. It knows what each thing it experiences means. Therefore, this world that is there in front of me and my own life has no distance from the self. In order to explain that the world as it exists is the result of an encounter between fact and consciousness, phenomenologists used to say that consciousness is *awareness of something* in order to say that we are intentionally linked to the world and our existence is linked to things and is taken as an object. When I think, I already think of something as an object, I don't think of emptiness. This is what Karl Jaspers explains in his *Introduction to Philosophical Thought:*

> What are we, these eyes that are in the world and see and know and understand? Thinking beings, we are the dimension - the only one, as far as we know - where that which is reveals itself in our objective thinking, in our understanding, in our actions, in every form of our experience.
> What's more, we only have awareness, but awareness of ourselves. In this awareness there is not only revelation, but the revelation of oneself to oneself. We've made a leap: we've gone from the intellectual cognition of objects to the subjective awareness of what we do and experience. The height we reach with this leap is nothing, if we consider it from the point of view of knowledge of the world; considered from a philosophical point of view, it is equivalent to the possibility of reaching a new awareness of being (JASPERS, 1993, p. 36).

The world in front of us is what appears to our consciousness, but it's not a jelly of nothingness. We don't know it in itself, because it is something that shows itself in contact with me, but it is more than its phenomenal appearance. And if reality surrounds us completely, it only seems to be what we can think of it, we haven't exhausted it, we've only achieved a personal understanding. Our relationship with what manifests itself is not free from our evaluations, feelings and perceptions. Everything that appears comes to me and I experience it in my own way. In this sense, each person's truth is fundamental, because it can reveal things that only that consciousness was capable of perceiving. However, because we can share experiences and information, we can build spaces of objectivity for the culturally defined manifestations of truth, such as those of religion, science, philosophy and our own very personal truths. Those that we hold dear as our most cherished reasons for living.

When we build bridges to the future in the realization of our existential freedom, we enter the terrain of belief, as Ortega said, because that is where we feel safe. When we lose confidence in the belief that gives us security, we enter a crisis. When I decide to become a professional, I need to be convinced that the profession I have chosen is reasonable, that we can do important work with it, that we can survive with dignity and be happy practicing it. In transcendence towards the future, then, belief is interconnected with freedom and the hope of realizing what is planned. Freedom is linked to changing the future and the hope that feeds it, but for freedom and hope to be realities in our lives we need to be open to the world itself. We need to understand that the construction of meaning takes place in culture.

When you lose hope, you lose the tenacity to go into the future, you lose the charm of the new. The baker whose story we summarized above was plunged into bitterness because he could find nothing but unhappiness in the future: he lived in a routine and superficial job that didn't seduce him, in the deprivation of being a widower without love and a father without recognition, in the financial limitations of the activity he practiced, in the distance from society that he didn't understand. Worst of all, he had no hope to guide him out of this existential mire in which he was immersed.

A human existence is an experience of freedom and of conquering the future.

10 Recognizing dignity

One of the challenges of our time is dealing with human dignity and making its effects felt in practice. Not that it's difficult to find reasons to justify it, not that dignity isn't fundamental, but the explanations of a globalized world end up not producing the effects when: fragmented economic activity doesn't facilitate such recognition, religious fundamentalisms don't stimulate criticism of sacred texts, mystical faith gains strength and vast areas fail to incorporate the notion of dignity. The exacerbation of desires and eroticism with subliminal advertising, the media's claim that material success is synonymous with happiness and meaning, also contributes to human dignity being little considered in our time.

It is well known that, as an ideal, dignity will never be perfectly lived, even if we all recognize its importance. However, as a value, dignity remains important and needs to be gradually recognized in order to produce its effects. And why has dignity been consolidated in the West and not elsewhere?

Due to the singularities of its cultural evolution. Throughout Western history, the reasons for this dignity have been presented and discussed. In the Christian perspective that accepts the incarnation of the Son of God, the dignity of man is elevated to the highest degree, since God himself became man and dwelt among us. The human condition has been elevated above animality. Incarnate Jesus of Nazareth, who in the Christian faith is the Son of God, left his divine condition to take on a human body. He then experienced our frailties and pain, leaving as a lesson love. He taught us that caring for other people is the best way to reach God. In doing so, he dignified the human condition by bringing man into the divine family. He taught that the most significant thing in relationships between people is the encounter of merciful love expressed in service to other people. And the most extraordinary teaching of Christianity is that love for other people is no different from love for God.

In the seventh chapter of his *Introduction to Theological Ethics*, Ronaldo Zacarias deals with *human rights* as a concrete expression of the dignity that the Christian faith has popularized. He says that human rights express in a concrete way the dignity that Christianity proclaims, but that in order for this dignity to be effective (2015, p. 139): "it needs to be converted into legal-political positives." The thesis, formulated in this way, does not seem accurate, because dignity does not necessarily need to be expressed in law in order to be valid. Nor does its placement in the law ensure that it will be effectively complied with, since the reasons for dignity are of a moral nature. However, the author is right to say that the recognition of human dignity by international organizations, imposed by Western countries, was expressed in legal statutes and eventually systematized in the UN declaration. The legal path is part of the concept's historical trajectory. The consensus that the author of the chapter says is universal is more properly speaking Western. It doesn't seem to have any real effect in some regions of the planet, such as those parts of Africa and Asia where radical Islamic law is in force, or even in China, a society that has opened up to capitalism, but not to the other realities of the West.

Dignity is a historical achievement in ethics. Various laws and Constitutions of Western nations are concerned with safeguarding human dignity. Ronaldo Zacarias repeats Noberto Bobbio when he says that the 1948 *Universal Declaration of Human Rights* (UN) is the greatest global consensus on values. There's no denying that there's a great deal of agreement, but there hasn't really been a consensus, i.e. everyone's agreement. It is true that for a large part of humanity the notion of dignity was already well established in the last century, that man has a different and greater value than things. Zacarias points out that this is a historical novelty, in the sense that there has previously been no document expressing such universal recognition. Faced with this reality, he develops enlightening positions on what is important for all people to have their dignity recognized. And if the laws were inspired by Christian teachings, it seems reasonable to him that Christians should expect the laws to express human dignity and (2015, p. 142): "be more concerned with the rights of others than with their own." In this way, what he is doing is an ethical reading of the legal principle. Let's go back to the initial point: the issue is essentially an ethical one, because freedom cannot be left aside. Being free, the individual needs to recognize the dignity of others as an intimate demand, an internal obligation and not because of a legal norm. If dignity is seen as a legal obligation, it leaves freedom aside. Realistically, however, the author of the chapter notes that since dignity is an ideal, it is often difficult to realize moral values in life. So he proposes a meta-ethical sense as a guide to life, a sense that gives us direction so that we are not (id., p. 131) "the playthings of circumstances and opportunities and even of our own whims and desires." He also defends the need to use freedom (ibid): "to the extent that we educate ourselves to listen to the calls of our own human nature." Thus, understood as an ideal that guides the inner consciousness, it is possible to accept it. Otherwise, it would appear to be pharisaism, since it would eliminate the intimate demand in a legalistic reading.

The fact that Ronaldo Zacarias points to the ideal nature of value is proof that the legitimacy of the person is to be found in the ethical sphere and not in the law. Living in a tradition that pits positivism against legal idealism, it seems to me that both attitudes are not the best way to deal with the problem. However, since there is an insurmountable link between ethics and law, to the extent that law is able to take on part of the value it expresses in the law, then laws can contain a moral value. Finally, in order to make Ronaldo Zacarias' thesis more precise, it seems important to take it as the concretization of personalism and axiological historicism in that form of three-dimensionalism of Law that Miguel Reale spoke of. For the Brazilian philosopher, fact, value and legal norm are inseparable. This is different from positing an ethical value. As shown in *Miguel Reale, ethics and the philosophy of law:*

> In Miguel Reale's understanding, man is a person. This represents a way of considering man that draws on the humanist tradition of Western philosophy. The theoretical instrument for this is Kantism, as indicated above, although the dialogue with Kant requires overcoming *apriorist* formalism, which, according to Reale, will be done through dialogue with Hegel and Husserl. This dialogue does not mean adherence to their theses, but a new and unique construction based on them (CARVALHO, 2011, p. 156).

The text above draws attention to the theoretical justification of the notion of person. As a value, dignity was proposed by Christianity, but it was justified by philosophers. Justification always seems fundamental, because we think in order to act. Today, dignity is not just a religious proposal, it is also a construct of ethics. Several contemporary philosophers have dealt with the subject, and it is enough to remember two with whom

Miguel Reale dialogued: Max Scheler and Ortega y Gasset. The former thought of values in general, including dignity, as a historical construction, while the latter placed values among the responses of lived reason to the problems we face. We are rational, but not an abstract rationality. If we understand rational man, it is a personified reason that chooses in the circumstances in which it finds itself.

What has been said points to the fact that we cannot think of human dignity apart from the notion of value. And this value, as Emmanuel Kant began to elaborate in his *Critique of Practical Reason,* is an expression of the spirit. It is practical reason that recognizes the value of the person and discovers something beyond what is in common with animals. Kant said:

> The second view, on the other hand, exalts my value as an intellect through my personality, in which the moral law reveals to me a life independent of animality and even of all the sensible world, because it can interfere in the determination, according to an end established by this law for my existence, a determination that is not limited to the conditions and limits of this life, but extends to infinity. (KANT, 1985, p. 802)

The theoretical justifications for the value of the person go back to patristics and medieval studies of the relationship between the divine persons. The concept of person was initially used to refer to the relationship between Christ and the Father, and between both and the Holy Spirit. It was on the basis of theological studies that Boecio constructed his notion of person as a rational substance with an individual nature and Descartes, in modern times, treated it as a conscious Self. In these cases, the notion of person applied to man did not contain the same elements as divine persons. In the 18th century, Emmanuel Kant affirmed that man could not be treated as a means to other ends, but was an end in himself. He justified the dignity of man by its intersubjective nature. Although it is an ancient theme, the dignity of man needed to be re-signified in the 20th century, because positivist scientism, psychoanalysis, Marxist socialism and analytic philosophy itself bypassed this intellectual tradition. That's why we highlight the contributions of Max Scheler, Ortega y Gasset and Miguel Reale, because these authors put the value of man back into practice.

The concept of personal dignity, which in patristics emphasized the individuality and interpenetration of the Divine Persons, incorporated the idea of personal conscience and freedom in modern times with Descartes and Kant. In the latter case, the concept began to refer to man and not to God.

In the last century, the idea of dignity began to draw on historicity, because the value of man also lies in the fact that he is not the first man, but that he draws on the experiences and learning of past generations to make something new, more complex, better conceived and also better. This is how dignity has been conceived at different times in history. All aspects relating to the person as a value have entered into the characterization of man and his distinction from other beings, as in Reale's formula, man is a *being who must be.*

The study of the human person as a reality of value needs to be taken up again at the beginning of the 21st century. Why? Firstly, because the process of globalization of the world economy has taken on new elements with the communications revolution. We are witnessing the acceleration of global economic relations. These relations became visible with the great navigations of Portugal and Spain in the 15th and 16th centuries. The process is old, its novelty is its acceleration.

With the development of communication technologies, the formation of agencies and corporations and the increasing use of communication satellites, the exchange of information has increased dramatically. You also have real-time news of what's happening anywhere in the world and you can apply it to stock exchanges all over the world. You apply it today on one and tomorrow on another. This revolution in communications has favored the fragmentation of the production process and its dispersion across different regions.

There is something important to consider. Trade in this global market, with its value chains, is not a purely economic phenomenon; it also affects other aspects of the cultural world. It popularizes artists, music, films, tastes, etc. In this way, each nation tries to reorganize the cultural elements that identify it and tries to resignify the cultural products that come from the more developed regions. However, this cultural movement takes little account of the dignity of the individual. Certain media programs, which are repeated on televisions all over the world, are limited to banal entertainment.

Today's society, which is born out of these relations of production in multinational companies, generally doesn't take care of the relations of solidarity that used to exist between national and local groups. In a way, they weaken the poorest states, just at a time when the churches have given weak answers to man and his suffering and clubs and organizations have done nothing about it. Without a state that takes care of this social area by offering good schools, the opportunity to take care of health, supplementary food programs and affordable housing, the lives of these populations degenerate. Without concrete action, the discourse of dignity sinks into emptiness. Although these aspects alone do not guarantee the dignity of those living in poverty, much less do they guarantee that the man of today will have a caring look at the suffering of others, because the recognition of dignity needs practical ways of realization, without which it becomes an empty discourse.

The new family, which is organized and presented differently from the traditional one, as we have already mentioned, shows another aspect of the challenge of dignity. If it seems inappropriate to use religious and transcendent categories to explain human relationships, to say that human marriage is similar to the marriage of Christ and the Church, for example, it cannot mean that we can disregard the lives of its members. We are left with the challenge of allowing everyone to find their own way, to establish a respectful and caring relationship with people who are not of the same blood, to discover and share love and understanding in these new families. All this strengthens the dignity of the person.

Moral and work training is often lacking in the preparation of children. Until a few decades ago, the father's profession was taught to his children, who generally followed it. Moral behavior was the responsibility of the Church, but in the world of global value chains and Churches that don't touch man's problems, both things have become out of reach for families. The school has a role to play in this process, but it is unable to provide an effective response, leaving the media in charge of these fundamental teachings. And the models that the media presents as symbols of success and happiness are artists, models or footballers. They are all millionaires, whose reality is far removed from that of almost everyone else, but who dictate fashion and the ideal of life. It's a fragile model, with little consistency, but it has a great impact on young people who adopt it without criticism.

Our challenge is to rebuild personal relationships, in families, social groups, churches and schools, so that the essential fundamental values of the civilized world, including dignity, find ways of being conveyed. A dignity that comes from the responsible use of freedom, from the development of personal meaning based on self-discovery, from responsible relationships. In short, there is the challenge of intimately retracing the path of dignity.

This is the faith that drives the Christian West and which has gained depth through philosophical debate. Love for the other is what takes us out of ourselves, what takes us beyond ourselves in a wonderful experience of transcendence. And even in the Christian faith, the other is never absolutely other, because we are companions in destiny. These aspects oblige us to recognize them as equal in dignity. An equal who is different in so many things that make him or her unique, but who is equal in common humanity, in the possibility of choosing responsibly.

When we see attacks like those that took place in Paris in November 2015, which killed more than a hundred people and injured almost three hundred, we realize that respect for dignity is far from widespread, because in doing so we give others the right to life, to a fair trial, to keep their faith, to choose their profession, etc. No one is bound by anything other than the law. Discovering the reasons for dignity in reason, in historical debate and outside religious fundamentalism, is a challenge that the people of our time have yet to overcome.

11 A word of farewell

It's not uncommon to hear people say that they're running out of time to do something or that it's simply over and there's still so much to do. A student who has dedicated years of his life to his university education and is now about to graduate says that there was still a lot to learn. At first, amid expectations and hopes, he thought it would take him a long time to finish his degree, but one day he wakes up in the morning and realizes that the course is over, that his classmates are gone, that he will no longer have classes, that he will no longer see his teachers and that he must work. And this discovery doesn't end there, with the same surprise he once experienced, he realizes a few years later that ten years have passed since the day he graduated, then twenty, thirty, and he reaches retirement wondering how much there was still to do in the world of work that hadn't been done. His children have grown up, are now parents themselves and have their own challenges in a world that is no longer his. And there was still so much to be done to form them before they went on to adulthood. Life brings this feeling of incompleteness, the feeling of incompleteness multiplies in existence.

At some point in life, if we don't die young, we discover that we belong to a generation that is leaving the scene and that another has taken its place. That familiar world is no longer the same and we need to learn different things from those that were necessary when we were young. This feeling that there is still something to do and say, that we don't want to leave the scene just yet, but that new demands are being placed on us at every moment, is part of human life. We live in time and with the feeling that we never have enough of it to do everything that needs to be done. Everything goes by extremely quickly and before we know it, time is up. Even if we dedicate ourselves a lot, there will still be a lot to do and if we don't dedicate ourselves as much, the emptiness left by the unlived will be greater.

That's the feeling we experience when we give the final word. I've said some things, we've dealt with essential issues for today's man, but there's always the feeling that there's still a lot to say, even though the pages no longer fit. The time comes when we have to give the final word. In everything, the final word comes with the realization of incompleteness. It is part of our finitude to come face to face with the end.

We're talking about things that have happened to us and that reflect the experience of a certain period of time, of a short century like the last one, which ended around 1988, and of another that began later and that we don't know how it will end. And in this same movement we have opened a new millennium of which we have already completed almost two decades. There are those who say that it is better to keep quiet about some of the subjects mentioned here, because we have little to say about what cannot be demonstrated. With regard to the experience of God, for example, we are always left with the inevitable doubt as to whether it would have been better not to speak at all, because we are treating a Being as the object of our consciousness that is not suitable for this. We know little about God beyond our faith. God is therefore a special subject for our intelligence, an impenetrable and fascinating challenge.

However, the man of this time cannot stop talking about God, because we live in a time when people kill in His name and the globalized world brings religious beliefs into close contact. These differences still lead to conflicts, not like the wars of the Middle Ages, but still violent conflicts. We also know that there were many deaths due to the repression of the truths of faith, but we also know that these truths hid political and group interests. Our time is an era in which bombs are exploded in public places, beheadings are carried out in front of cameras, people are set on fire live and atrocities are broadcast on the world wide web. The impression always remains that such barbarities have something more cruel, more absurd than what we have experienced in other times. Objectively, they may not, but this perception is due to the fact that such things are more clearly irrational and contrary to any meditated experience of God.

Our formulations about God, like our reflections on the truth of philosophy, are imprecise and only improve through communication and personal encounters. Only by sharing our experience of these topics can we overcome the errors present in our inevitable limitation. Making mistakes is part of our finitude. We make mistakes when we choose a profession, when we choose friends, when we give our hearts to an unlikely love, but we don't get any smaller from our mistakes if we recognize them, if we learn to get up when we fall and move forward making the best of our limitations. Learning to deal with the mistakes and pitfalls of existence is a great thing that is not often talked about.

When my generation finished high school in the mid-1970s, we had the feeling that the world would always be divided between the capitalist West and the communist East. And the Soviet Union, which seemed like a solid edifice, crumbled like a sand castle. We used to believe in moral progress and the betterment of mankind. The 20th century brought the collapse of all the romantic dreams of the *belle epoque* and ended up taking with it a world we thought was unshakeable. We had lived our youth in the expectation that it could end at any moment through the insane act of some unbalanced leader or general. Jaspers repeats Einstein's words close to his death in 1955. And in his words in *The Atomic Bomb and the Future of Man* we find the spirit of those days:

> The great physicists, whose intellectual capacity made this new reality possible, inform us about this. In 1955, shortly before his death, Einstein, along with others, signed a moving appeal, which read: in the event of the mass use of hydrogen bombs, we must expect the instantaneous death of part of humanity and the painful illness and consequent death of all living beings (JASPERS, 1958, p. 12-13).

Since the fall of the Berlin Wall, this reality seems to have evaporated, although all the bombs are still there and could fall into the hands of terrorists. And the world is no longer divided into two large blocs. Without them, local conflicts have exploded with a violence we never imagined. And if left unchecked, these conflicts will begin to occur, and with the global scale of events on the computer network, local problems will be taken to all corners of the world. And conflicts in the Islamic world have also exploded with seemingly uncontrollable force.

Just as tragic as the actions of terrorists is the commercialization of drugs in all countries and the growth of organized crime. These realities, which also appear in more developed countries, take on dramatic proportions in underdeveloped countries. This is because in poor countries there are endless numbers of young people willing to take on the risks of the drug trade, because they find in it a source of income that is impossible for them to earn in any other way, either because they are experiencing family breakdown and personal poverty, or because they are seduced by the great consumerism.

Wandering the streets of the great cities of the underdeveloped world, the crowd of miserable addicts shows the harshest face of human degradation. People who add the most extreme poverty to the greatest indignity, willing to do anything, from murder to prostitution, for a bit of drugs.

From what has been said, there are two possible certainties: history is heading in an unpredictable direction, even though man has his sights set on building a better society. This is a desire or dream built in the sphere of morality for which humanity strives. The other certainty is that in the midst of the crisis of great change, each person is left with the task of living with excellence. It is necessary for everyone to find a reason to live in accordance with themselves and to transform this reason into a search for life.

REFERENCES

CARVALHO, Jose Mauricio de. **O Homem e a Filosofia, pequenas meditates sobre a existencia e a cultura**. 2. ed., Porto Alegre: Edipucrs, 2007.

. **Ethics**. Sao Joao del-Rei: UFSJ, 2010.

. **Miguel Reale, ethics and philosophy of law**. Porto Alegre: Edipucrs, 2011.

DESCARTES, Rene. **Discourse on Method**. Sao Paulo: Hemus, 1978.

FRANKL, Victor. **The question of meaning in psychotherapy**. Campinas: Papirus, 1990.

GARAUDY, Roger. **Word of Man**. Sao Paulo: Difel, 1975.

JASPERS, Karl. **The atomic bomb and the future of man**. Rio de Janeiro: Agir, 1958.

. **Scientific Initiation**. Lisbon: Guimaraes, 1987.

. **Introduction to philosophical thought**. 9. ed., Sao Paulo: Cultrix, 1993.

LIPOVETSKY, Gilles and SERROY, Jean. **World culture; response to a disoriented society**. Sao Paulo: Companhia das Letras, 2011.

KANT, Emmanuel. The Critique of Practical Reason. **Philosophical works**. Paris: Gallimard, 1985.

KUJAWSKI, Gilberto de Mello. **Living and dangerous**. Sao Paulo: GDR, 1986.

ORTEGA Y GASSET, Jose. The rebellion of the masses. **Obras Completas**. 2ª reprint, v. IV, Madrid: Alianza, 1994.

. Ensimismamiento y alteracion. **Obras Completas**. 2nd reprint, v. V, Madrid: Alianza, 1994.

. What is Philosophy? **Obras Completas**. 2nd reprint, v. VII, Madrid: Alianza, 1997.

. The idea of principle in Leibniz and the evolution of deductive theory. **Obras Completas**. 2nd reprint, v. VIII, Madrid: Alianza, 1994.

TRASFERETTI, Jose Antonio; MILLEN, Maria Inez de Castro and ZACARIAS, Ronaldo. **Introduction to theological ethics**. Sao Paulo: Paulus, 2015.

MIX
Papier aus verantwortungsvollen Quellen
Paper from responsible sources
FSC® C105338

Printed by Books on Demand GmbH, Norderstedt / Germany